Lindemann Group
PETER SCHIESSL

CorelDRAW 2020

TRAINING BOOK WITH MANY EXERCISES

*Something looks different?
Use Window/Workspace/Default*

ISBN 979-8635639-30-6
Print on Demand since April, 09th 2020
Lindemann Group
© Dipl.-Ing. (FH) Peter Schiessl
Fortnerstr. 8, 80933 Munich, Germany
webmaster@kamiprint.de
www.kamiprint.de
www.lindemann-beer.com
All rights prohibited.
Any use of pages or sentences of this book without written permission
of the author is a violation of international law and copyright.
Place of court is Munich.

This book is made with great accuracy, but neither author nor publisher
can take any liability for damages caused by mistakes in this book or in
the programs described in this book. Alterations of content or price of
this book reserved.

Some names and product names are registered trade names of
other companies. The usage of this book as a training manual for
the original product is not in conflict with
international trade names prohibitions.

Table of Contents

1. Principles — 7
- 1.1 The Corel-Family (Samples) 7
- 1.2 Workspace 8
- 1.3 Preliminary Considerations 8

2. Vector or Pixel? — 9
- 2.1 CorelDRAW or Photo-Paint 9
- 2.2 Vector-Graphics 9
- 2.3 Photos are Pixel-Graphics 10
- 2.4 By Comparison 11
- 2.5 Division of labor in practice 11
- 2.6 The File Types 12
  - 2.6.1 Theory File Endings 12
  - 2.6.2 Show File Extensions 13
  - 2.6.3 Convert data types 13
  - 2.6.4 Example File Extensions 14
- 2.7 The Window "Hints" 15

TO DRAW 17
with rectangles, ellipses, lines, colors 17

3. First Steps — 19
- 3.1 Start Corel 19
- 3.2 The Drawing Functions at a Glance 20
- 3.3 Change, Move, Delete Rectangle 21
- 3.4 Rectangle Rotate or Distort 21
  - 3.4.1 Selection 22
- 3.5 Move and Copy 22
- 3.6 The Property Bar 24
- 3.7 To Save 24

4. Ellipses, Select, Colors — 25
- 4.1 The CorelDraw Construction 25
- 4.2 Set up the Page 26
- 4.3 Rectangles, Ellipses, Variety 26
- 4.4 Marking and Moving 27
- 4.5 Select Colors 28
- 4.6 The Color Palette 28
- 4.7 Changing Line Thickness 29
- 4.8 The Property Bar – Position 30
- 4.9 Undo 30
  - 4.9.1 Delete 30

5. Zoom and View — 31
- 5.1 Zoom with the Zoom Tool 31
- 5.2 The Zoom Button 32
- 5.3 Setting the Display 32
- 5.4 Settings of CorelDraw 33
- 5.5 Switch the Command Bars on or off 33

6. Lines — 35

- 6.1 Freehand Tool ... 35
  - 6.1.1 Straight Lines ... 35
  - 6.1.2 Polygon ... 35
- 6.2 Lines in an Angle ... 36
- 6.3 Exercise Lines ... 36
- 6.4 Exercise Convertible ... 36
- 6.5 Pencil Types ... 37
- 6.6 Artistic Media Tools ... 37
  - 6.6.1 Artistic Media Tools - Preset ... 37
  - 6.6.2 Artistic Media Tools - Brush ... 38
  - 6.6.3 Artistic Media Tools - Sprayer ... 38
  - 6.6.4 Artistic Media Tools - Calligraphic ... 38
- 6.7 Exercise Pen ... 39
- 6.8 Smart Fill Tool ... 39
- 6.9 Smart Drawing ... 39
- 6.10 Live Scetch ... 40

PRECISE DRAWING ... *41*
Square, Circle, Grid, Guidelines, Text, Group ... *41*

7. PRECISE DRAWING — 43

- 7.1 The Grid ... 43
  - 7.1.1 EXERCISE: PYRAMIDS FROM SQUARES ... 44
  - 7.1.2 FURTHER ON THE GRID ... 44
- 7.2 Copy and Move ... 45
- 7.3 Guidelines Setup ... 46
  - 7.3.1 Set Guidelines and Move ... 46
  - 7.3.2 The Guidelines-Menu ... 47
  - 7.3.3 Angled Guidelines-Menu ... 47
- 7.4 Aligning On ... 48
- 7.5 Exercise: Truck ... 48

8. Quadrates, Circles, Shapes — 49

- 8.1 Quadrates and Circles ... 49
  - 8.1.1 Exercise: Quadrates and Circles with Guidelines and Grid 50
- 8.2 Polygon, Spiral, Grinding ... 51
- 8.3 Common Shapes: Basic, Arrow, Flowchart etc. ... 51

9. Ruler, Zero Point, Group — 53

- 9.1 Ruler and Zero Point ... 53
- 9.2 Exercise: Railway Wheel ... 54
- 9.3 The Menu "Transform" ... 55
- 9.4 Group Objects ... 56
  - 9.4.1 Exercise: Blossom ... 56

10. Text and Symbols — 57

- 10.1 Text Editing in Corel ... 57
  - 10.1.1 Text Formatting with the Property Bar ... 57
  - 10.1.2 Modify Text with the Pick Tool ... 58
- 10.2 Exercise: Solar ... 59
- 10.3 The Symbol Fonts ... 60

COLORS 61
Fillings, ClipArt, Photos 61

11. Single Fillings — 63
- 11.1 Overview select Filling and adjust 63
- 11.2 Modify the Preset 64
- 11.3 The Color Palette 64
- 11.4 Color Settings 65
- 11.5 Color Palettes 66

12. Fountain Fill — 67
- 12.1 Adjust the Fountain Fill 68
- 12.2 Multiple Color Filling 69
- 12.3 Exercise: Christmas Card 70
- 12.4 Exercise: Carton home 72
- 12.5 Exercise: Steam Locomotive 73

13. Special Fillings — 75
- 13.1 Full Color Fillings 75
- 13.2 Bitmap-Pattern Fillings 76
- 13.3 Two-Color Filling 76
- 13.4 Texture Fill – the CorelDraw Fillings 76
- 13.5 Postscript Patterns 77
- 13.6 The tile size 78
- 13.7 Make a New Pattern Fill 78
- 13.8 Copy a Filling 78

14. ClipArt and Shadow — 79
- 14.1 Insert ClipArt or Photos 79
- 14.2 The Corel-Objects 80
- 14.3 Exercise: Birthday Invitation 81
  - 14.3.1 Background for whole Page 81
  - 14.3.2 Shadow Tool 82
- 14.4 Insert ClipArt 83

15. Interactive Menus — 85
- 15.1 Interactive Fill Pattern 85
- 15.2 Interactive Mesh Fill 86
- 15.3 Interactive Transparency 87
- 15.4 Inserting Photos 88

16. Curve Editing — 91
- 16.1 Exercise: Party 91
- 16.2 The Stars – Move the Turn Points 92
- 16.3 The Moon - Circle Segments 92
- 16.4 Combine to Fill 94
- 16.5 Closing of the Figure 94
- 16.6 Add Turnpoints for the Nose 95
- 16.7 The Figures – Adapt their Shape 96

17. The Snake – Curves Total — 99
- 17.1 First Preliminary Exercise 100
- 17.2 Second Preliminary Exercise 101
- 17.3 Serious Case: The Snake 102

| 17.4 The Head and the Points | 103 |

18. Text Editing — 105
18.1 PRODUCING SHADOWS	105
18.2 Insert Special Characters	107
18.3 Color Variety	107
18.4 Align Text to an Object	107
18.5 Add The Address	108
18.6 Other Adjustments for Text	108
18.7 Other Text Helps	110

19. The Paragraph Text — 111
19.1 Converting Text	111
19.2 Exercise: Business Card	112
19.3 Handling with the Paragraph Text Frames	113
19.4 Print from CorelDraw	114

20. Pictures and Text — 115
20.1 Insert Photos	116
20.2 Cut Edge Areas of Photos	116
20.3 Insert Paragraph Text	117
20.4 Text Formatting and Hyphenation	117
20.5 Add a Page	118
20.6 Edit Photos	119

EFFECTS — 121
for Text and Extrusion ... 121

21. Effects for Text — 123
21.1 Interactive Effects	123
21.2 Move Letters	124
21.3 Add Perspective	124
21.4 The Envelope Effect	125
21.5 Contour	126

22. Extrusion — 127
22.1 The Depth of the Extrusion	127
22.2 The Color	128
22.3 The Rotation	128
22.4 Light and Shadow	129
22.5 Bevels	129
22.6 A Title Sheet	130
22.7 Exclusion Exercise: Extrusion	131
22.8 SUMMARY SHADOWS	131
22.9 Basics	132

23. Index — 133

1. PRINCIPLES

In this book, we systematically describe CorelDRAW from the beginning and with many exercises. But to use this book and the powerful CorelDRAW program, you must have some prerequisites: general computer and **Windows basics,** e.g. **experience** drawing with mouse and keyboard, **Windows basics**: how to save files, open, rename, and copy files to a USB stick or to another folder.

That way, you will avoid frustrations and have much more fun with computers and this computer graphic course.

1.1 THE COREL-FAMILY (SAMPLES)

The download is part of a package. Here a short presentation of the parts of this package.

The main content of CorelDRAW Suite:

- ◆ **CorelDRAW** is the vector-based program for graphics, design work, posters, presentations, business cards and more.
  - ✎ Most functions of Corel PHOTO-PAINT for photos are integrated into CorelDRAW so the switch to PHOTO-PAINT is mostly not necessary.
- ◆ **Corel PHOTO-PAINT** is for working with photos. Photos in the computer are created by scanning or taking with a digital photo camera, which are saved point for point (pixel = picture elements).

After the installation, you'll find on your desktop, these symbols:

The main programs:
CorelDRAW: the drawing program and **Photo-Paint** the photo program.

More Add-Ins: **Capture** (Create pictures from the screen) and the **Font Manager** (Manage fonts), **Duplexing Wizard** – depending on the version are not always included.

1. Ch.: Principles — CorelDRAW 2020

More Add-Ins:

- **Corel Connect** is a utility that provides online clip art and photos from Corel, and in addition, you can search for images in online photo libraries, e.g. at Flickr.
  - With Corel 2020, Connect is no longer a custom icon, it can only be started via **Window/Dockers/Connect**.

Using the "**Launch**" symbol, you can start installed apps and plug-ins or download more additional apps and plug-ins:

- Corel BARCODE WIZARD
- Corel CAPTURE
- Corel Font Manager
- Corel PHOTO-PAINT
- CorelDRAW
- Corel AfterShot HDR
- Get More...

According to your version of Corel and installation, it is possible to have more or fewer apps than are in this list!

Here you can install more addons, some of them are freeware.

1.2 Workspace

When starting for the first time, a **Welcome Screen** appears there you can choose the workspace, **Lite**, **Default** or **Touch** or by **Speciality Illustration**, **Page Layout** and **Adobe Illustrator**:

- Depending on your choice, the icons and commands are arranged slightly differently.
- In the following we will use the working area "**Default**", the usual setting.
  - **Lite** is more reduced with as few symbols as possible, **Touch** is optimized for devices with touch-sensitive screens.
- You can choose the workspace anytime by the command Window/Workspace.

Looks different? Use Window/Workspace/Default

1.3 Preliminary Considerations

A good cook cooks to the taste of his customers. Similarly, to decide if your graphic work is good, you must consider if it matches your customers' needs. So, think first about your target group.

Some suggestions:

- Advertisement for a music festival or business company?
- Birthday party for child turning 4 or 14 years old, or for a company event?

Generally, you can say that a younger customer enjoys more colorful and crazier designs.

Today, many people have very good color laser printers, but they are not good enough for a professional advertisement.

2. Vector or Pixel?

CorelDRAW is a **vector drawing** program, while Corel PHOTO-PAINT stores the images as **pixel graphics**.

2.1 CorelDRAW or Photo-Paint

Why **CorelDRAW**, why **Corel Photo-Paint**? In practice, most times both programs are useful because they complete each other.

- **Photo-Paint** is for working with photos. Photos on the computer are so-called pixel-pictures because, simply, photos are created dot by dot, and the color of each dot is saved.
- **CorelDRAW** is used to make graphic works with prepared photos, text and clipart's such as presentation charts, promotion sheets or business cards/logos.

This working separation results from the big difference between both programs, similar to the difference between photos and drawings. This will be explained below.

2.2 Vector-Graphics

With vector graphics, drawn elements (lines, circles, rectangles ...) are stored as mathematic functions (vectors): Line from point $x1$, $y1$ to $x2$, $y2$ with line width and line color.

For a line, therefore, the coordinate of the start and end point is noted, in addition to the line thickness, color and type.

- For this reason, each drawn element can be subsequently resized or moved.
- Even with an enormous magnification, the lines always remain sharp.

In addition to CorelDRAW, there are numerous other vector-oriented programs, and therefore some different **file extensions** are used.

> Of course, all CAD programs are also vector programs (CAD = computer-aided design = computer-aided drawing, programs for technical drawing).

2.3 Photos are Pixel-Graphics

Similar to the screen, a picture is composed of many points. The color is stored for each of these **dots (or pixels)**. Your screen might display the image with 1920 horizontal and 1080 vertical points (= Full HD resolution) - depending on the settings of your monitor.

This explains why image files become quite large and the following problem arises: **small file - poor image quality** or **good picture quality - large file.**

If pixel images of poor quality are increased, the dots are clearly visible. Instead of straight lines, stairs are recognizable as on old dot matrix printers.

Overview pixel-graphics

White dots: the edge area, which is not registered by us, is stored point by point, too!

Green dots.

Black dots for the line.

Magenta dots.

Pixel-Ball

Pixel-letter.

Compressing (Simplified explanation):

- When photos have large areas with small color differences, such as blue skies, high compression is possible:
  - Here, the compression function can be used to reduce the file size: instead of AAABBBBBCCCC, a formula can store this shorter as "3A5B4C".
  - In addition, other methods are employed, e.g. a reduction of the details and color differences and dividing into blocks that are 8x8 points each.
- Drawbacks:
  - Each time you load or save, the computer must calculate the compression.
  - A low-quality loss arises because the original image is slightly changed. This difference in quality, however, only occurs at higher compression rates above 20:1.

The best compression comes from the .jpg file format, which has therefore become the standard format for photos. In PHOTO-PAINT **file-save as** and select as jpg as the file type.

jpg

2.4 BY COMPARISON

The differences between the two formats explain the advantages and disadvantages.

Advantages of vector graphics (CorelDRAW):

- Small files with **sharp**, precise lines and edges.
- Objects (e.g., rectangle, circle) can be **changed** as desired.
- Special **effects** are possible, e.g. adding shadow to a text.

For that, still pixel graphics (Photo-Paint)?

- Pixel graphics are an unavoidable evil because a **scanner** scans line-by-line, dot-by-dot, saving the color of each dot.
  - Also, a **digital camera** stores the pixel by dot, e.g. from 18 million points per image.
  - Thus, **all digital photos are pixel images**.
- Another application case for a pixel program is **painting as with a brush** and color on a canvas. Many advertising graphics use this effect e.g. for pseudo-children's pictures.

Paint as with brush and paint on canvas

goes in Corel Photo-Paint: everything is painted over, which is why, as in nature, the previous state can not always be restored.

However, the border CorelDRAW to Corel Photo-Paint runs smoothly. **Detailed painting** to drawing, e.g. a wintery house with snow on the roof and smoky chimney, is already more useful in CorelDRAW because it can be corrected and changed at any time, and because e.g. a window is drawn only once, then copied as often as required, and Photo-Paint is to correct and prepare **photos** or copy an object out of a photo to use in a CorelDraw presentation.

2.5 DIVISION OF LABOR IN PRACTICE

- First, prepare the pictures or photos in **PHOTO-PAINT**:
  - Scan or edit images (cut out objects, correct brightness, etc.)
- Then, complete the presentation in **CorelDRAW**:
  - Load images, add text and custom drawing elements.
- Consider **advertising**: there are photos (photo-paint) combined with other background and text (CorelDRAW).

For CorelDRAW	For PHOTO-PAINT (Pixel)
Presentations	Scan and edit images (for example, correct brightness, cut away edges).
Leaflets	Edit photos (for example, create an image section).
Title pages	Paint or modify images or clipart in pixel format.
Painting (detailed)	Painting like children.
Drawings	Cut objects from photos (e.g. a person. This object can be inserted into other files or photos).
Business cards etc.	

In PHOTO-PAINT, if possible, do not add text as text is converted into pixel patterns and cannot be changed afterwards. It is better to only edit pure photos in PHOTO-PAINT and add texts only in CorelDRAW.

CorelDRAW is not designed for **text processing** on a large scale. With a lot of text, work this way: prepare the pictures in Photo-Paint, the graphics elements in CorelDRAW, and import the results to a modern word processing program and assemble with text (layout). If graphics elements are marked in Corel, they can be exported to the .wmf or .emf format, and then they can easily be inserted into all Microsoft programs.

2.6 THE FILE TYPES

2.6.1 THEORY FILE ENDINGS

There are many different drawing and painting programs. Each of these programs uses a specific file extension. Why?

- The file name can be up to 255 characters from Windows 95 onwards. Even empty keys and customary characters may be used, but no "\" (backslash, because it is used to separate folders).
- The file extension usually consists of three or four letters separated by a dot from the file name.
  - In addition, a symbol for each data type and an explanatory text, e.g. "Data Type CorelDRAW Graphics" is shown in Windows.
  - The file extension indicates the program with which a file was created.
- As an illustration:
  - Filename.cdr (cdr as file extension for CorelDRAW).
  - Filename.cpt (cpt as file extension for Corel Photo-Paint).

.
*.cdr
*.cpt

2.6.2 Show File Extensions

So, it's handy to see the file extensions. Since Windows 95, the file extensions are unfortunately no longer displayed automatically. A brief guide for Windows 10 on how to do this:

- Start the **Windows Explorer**, and open the options on the right side of the map view. In the menu that appears choose the map "View", and remove the mark by the option "**Hide extensions for known file types**"

2.6.3 Convert data types

Usually, files can only be edited further in the source program. But not with good graphics programs. In Corel, almost every picture or graphics file can be imported.

- In the standard installation, not all **import and export filters** are loaded! Possibly. re-install. To do this, start the Corel Setup again and reload the desired file formats.
- **ClipArt** and vector files should never be opened in PHOTO-PAINT as this means a loss of quality due to the conversion to pixel format.

> PHOTO-PAINT only for photos (=Pixel pictures),
> CorelDRAW for vector graphics!

2.6.4 EXAMPLE FILE EXTENSIONS

A certain knowledge of the file endings is useful to recognize the file identities:

File extensions for vector graphics (drawings, graphics)	
cdr	CorelDRAW-drawing.
ai	Adobe Illustrator file
eps	Encapsulated Postscript: standard format for vector graphics (Originally Adobe printer language).
dwg	AutoCAD-drawing (abbreviation of drawing).
wmf	Windows Metafile: a format used by Microsoft, therefore, can be used in MS programs (e.g. Word) as well as emf (enhanced metafile).

The **ClipArt** elements from the CorelDRAW package are also stored in the cdr format, like the CorelDRAW drawings, and could therefore also be drawn.

File extensions for pixel graphics (photos, painted pictures)	
cpt	Corel **Photo-Paint**-picture
pcx	Previously, many ClipArt files were stored in this formerly widespread format.
bmp	Bitmap: Windows background images were saved earlier in this format. Today they are rare, since there was no compression!
tif	Target Image File: Formerly standard format for scanned images.
gif	Graphic Image File: Good compression, therefore recommended for pixel graphics, but max. 256 colors, not enough for photos.
png	Portable Network Graphic: With no-loss compression.
pcd	Kodak-Photo-CD-Pictures: Excellent picture quality, accordingly large files. When copying to the hard disk, the desired quality of the image can be reduced accordingly.
jpg	Very good compression, therefore very recommendable, especially for a very large image being copied to the cloud. Meanwhile, it is the standard format for digital photos. Also, most digital cameras save in this format, usually with very high compression.
Jp2	JPEG2000 is the successor of jpg. Compression of jpg has been further improved, and additional information can be stored, e.g. recording date and recording settings, which may be useful for digital photo equipment.
raw	Without compression = without quality loss, used by professional photographers.

On the **Internet**, the transfer times are the problem, which is why pictures should be as small as possible: use jpg for photos going to the internet, and gif for drawn elements.

2.7 The Window "Hints"

A useful and helpful feature is the "**Notes**" window is displayed on the right.

There you will find information and instructions on the currently selected tool and you can read more detailed help texts with the hyperlinks shown below.

Use the X symbol to **close** this window, reopen with "Window/Dockers/Hints".

Now it is time to start our first drawing.

- Close with this X as all windows.
- Fold out / Unfold.
- Change to other open windows by clicking.
- Help texts on selected topics.
- Back to the homepage.
- Back / Forward.

➢ **Close** all open docking windows (on the right in the Corel), we do not need them for the time being and can open them again at **Window/Dockers** at any time.

First Part

To Draw

with rectangles, ellipses, lines, colors

---

*Looks different?
Use Window/Workspace/Default*

Chapter 3

3. First Steps

3.1 Start Corel

Start CorelDRAW from the start icon on the desktop or in the Windows start menu by CorelDRAW:

CorelDRAW will greet you with this welcome screen:

When you move the mouse over the headline, the X-symbol appears and you can close this welcome screen if you want to use the usual Windows icons for file reopening, opening or saving:

It can turned on again by the menu points **Window** and **Help/Welcome Screen"**.

Here you will find e.g. some explanatory videos and tutorials on learning, on "Get More" software, clip art collections and photos, currently, some of them for free.

Notice the symbols. Here you find the learning tools from Corel, e.g. some training videos.

Let us begin the first drawing:

- ➢ Select a **New Document** in one of the ways described.
  - ↳ Without the Welcome screen above, this is the same as in any other program with the icons at the top left (new / open).
- ➢ The appearing **window for preselection**, e.g. the drawing size, you can simply confirm with OK.

3.2 THE DRAWING FUNCTIONS AT A GLANCE

Before we start the drawing step by step, we first have a look at the **drawing tools** of Corel. These are located in the toolbox at the left edge:

- **Pick tool**: mark elements, change size or move.
- **Forming tool** for working with curve points.
- **Cut** the edges of a photo.
- **Zoom** to zoom in or out.
- **Pen** (freehand) for painting or drawing, also special pens are hidden here.
- **Artistic Media Tool**
- **Draw rectangles**
- **Circles** or ellipses.
- Draw a **polygon**, a spiral, a grid, or a finished shape: arrows, heart, etc.
- Write **text** or insert table.
- Add **dimensions**.
- Making **connections** (closing figures).
- Here the **effects** (shadow, fade, contour ...) are summarized.
- **Pipette**: Fill fillings and colors from the drawing.
- **Transparency effects**
- **Interactive Fill Tool**: fill options in the Property Bar. **Smart Fill Tool**: fast and easy filling with the mouse.
- For all functions with a **small triangle**, additional menus will pop up as soon as you click on them.

Looks different? Use Window-Workspace-Default

Note:

- If you place the mouse on a symbol for a short time, the **name** and a brief description of the function are reported. This is very convenient for orientation and searching for a suitable symbol.
- A **description** of the currently selected function is displayed in the Note window on the right side.
- If you want to **draw** something, first select the appropriate function (rectangle, line, etc.)!!
- If you want to **change** or adjust something, first select the desired object using **Pick Tool**.
  - ↳ Beginners often forget to switch to the pick tool and therefore draw many new mini-objects.
  - ↳ If you have drawn something inadvertently, undo it immediately, or delete it with the [Delete] key.

> Accidentally drawn miniature objects complicate the selection of other objects and are often only recognizable as errors during printing!

3.3 CHANGE, MOVE, DELETE RECTANGLE

A rectangle is best suited to explaining many character functions most easily. After drawing, all elements must be pushed to the correct position and adjusted to the correct size.

Try it:

- ➢ Select **Rectangle Tool**, then draw a rectangle with the mouse button held.
- ➢ Immediately switch to the **Pick Tool** so that new rectangles are not inadvertently drawn.

The **handle points** appear. When the handles are visible, the rectangle is highlighted and you can position the rectangle or modify its size:

At the **corner sizing handles,** both axes simultaneously increase or decrease.

Widen or change height.

Inside, on the line as well as on the cross in the middle, the rectangle can be **moved**.

When you switch to the **Shape Tool**, you can specify the rounding of the corners using the mouse.

- ➢ **Widen** the rectangle to the right.
- ➢ **Move** the rectangle.
- ➢ **Enlarge** the rectangle on both axes at a corner sizing handle.
- ➢ **Delete** the rectangle: selected elements can be deleted with the [Delete] key.

To edit:

- ♦ Click the element so that the **handle points** appear.
  - ✎ You can **change the size** at the touch points, or
  - ✎ Click and hold on the item and **move** it, or
  - ✎ **Delete** the selected part with [Delete].

3.4 RECTANGLE ROTATE OR DISTORT

Corel provides other highly useful and very easy to use functions, e.g. to make a **parallelogram** from a rectangle, or to **rotate** it.

- ♦ Use the **Pick Tool** to select the object for the first time:
  - ✎ The grip points appear where the size can be changed.
- ♦ Click on the object **again**:
  - ✎ **Arrows** appear. With the arrows at the corners you can **rotate**, with those in the middle you can **move parallel**.

> Draw a new **rectangle, switch** to the Pick Tool and click on it, that the rotation arrows appear:

The rectangle can be moved to a parallelogram with the **middle arrows**. Please try!

In the middle is a small circle, which represents the **pivot point**. You can move this point with the mouse e.g. to a corner to make a rotation around that vertex.

The rectangle can be **rotated** on the corner arrows. Pressing [Ctrl] at the same time rotates in 15 ° increments (exactly 15, 30, 45, 60, 90 degrees, etc.).

> Try all options, draw new rectangles if necessary.
> **Delete** all rectangles.

3.4.1 SELECTION

Some symbols like the rectangle have a **small triangle** on the lower right. A selection menu can then be opened by holding down the left mouse button. For the **3-point rectangle** you do not have to specify three points, but with the mouse button pressed, draw the first line, then click once and draw the second line.

3.5 MOVE AND COPY

Drawings are labour-intensive. For example, with a wheel for a car artistically drawn, you will want to copy it and not redraw it.

Copying in Corel is very easy with a little trick:

> Draw a **rectangle** again.

Always use the Pick Tool:

- Always use the **Pick Tool**. Press and hold the left mouse button on the rectangle, and you can move the rectangle.
- Hold down the left mouse button, **move** the rectangle the same way,
  - but on the way **a short click on the right mouse button** and the rectangle is **copied!**
  - When you **press the left mouse button**, you have enough time to push the copied rectangle to the desired position.

copy

➤ Create the following objects by **copying** them with the right mouse button as described above.

✎ If you hold down the [**Ctrl**] key, you can arrange the rectangles exactly horizontally or vertically.

Copying using the right mouse button is much easier than the normal way:

- **Select Object**, then **Edit/Copy**, the object is in memory, then **Edit/Paste** one or more copies or
- use the symbols:

Cut deletes the original.

The cut-out or copy can then be **Pasted** as often as desired.

Copy (the original is retained).

The keyboard shortcuts are another option:

[Ctrl]-X, C, V
[Ctrl]-D

- [**Ctrl**]-**X, C, V** for cut, copy or paste.
  ✎ **C** for **Copy** is easy to remember, the other buttons lie next to it. Otherwise, you can check the Edit Menu.

For making Duplicates you have some ways:

[Ctrl]-D

- With [**Ctrl**]-**D** or the Menu-Edit-**Duplicate** you get a copy.
  ✎ You can modify the duplicate distance anytime in the **Property Bar** if nothing is marked: 5.0 mm / 5.0 mm

Finishing the exercise:

➤ Finally, you can move the rectangle parallel and rotate as described above:

3.6 THE PROPERTY BAR

Note the **Property Bar**, which displays the most frequently required settings, depending on the selected object, for a rectangle,
e.g. the position, the size, the rounding of the corners.

You can change all values, e.g. the width from 2.276" to 2.3" and confirm with **Return** or a rounding with the arrows.

When you open the lock, you can set each corner individually.

3.7 TO SAVE

Our first exercise drawing should now be saved.

> Click on the symbol "Save".

We create a folder for our exercises. This goes directly in the **File Save** window by clicking "**New Folder**" (after you have chosen the left side the correct drive or folder in which you want to make a new folder, here "Documents"):

[Ctrl]-S

Save in the Corel Cloud, a new possibility by Version 2020.

We want to create a subfolder for our exercises in your "**Documents**" folder.

The "New Folder" appears here. Change its name, e.g. as "**Exercises CorelDRAW 2020**" or the course number, then confirm the name with Return and open the folder again with Return.

Only after the correct folder has been selected, enter the filename, e.g. "Exercise handles".

The **file extension .cdr** is complemented by Corel. The file transmission is not displayed by default in Windows. Graphics professionals should change this as on page 13, because with the help of the file endings, it is very easy to identify which software or photo program a file comes from.

Before each save, check these two important settings:

1. Is the correct **folder** selected above?
2. Does the extension fit the **file name**?
   - ↳ If you do not enter a **file extension** or a dot, Corel automatically supplements the ending **cdr**, or leave the suffix right: filename.**cdr**

cdr from CorelDRAW

After saving, the new file name is displayed at the top of the CorelDRAW bar.

4. Ellipses, Select, Colors

4.1 The CorelDraw Construction

At the top is the command menu **File ...**, selected commands as icons in the toolbar, and the Properties bar. Notice: this is with **workspace default**.

The commands, sorted into groups:
- Under **File**, all commands relating to the file: Save, Open...,
- Under **Edit**: Undo, Copy, etc.

Corel Window:
- minimize,
- full-image / small picture,
- close.

The **property bar** shows suitable settings for the selected object.

Switch between open windows and drawings.

Scroll bars to move the displayed image section.

The **Toolbox**:
Symbols to switch to the desired character functions, e.g. line or rectangle, circle or text, adjust colors, pen thickness ...

Left: the painting area is indicated by a sheet of paper.
Right: the Hints window.

Rulers allow precise work.

The **color** can be selected here.

➢ Close the **Dockers Windows** with the X, they consume too much space. You can turn them on again with **Window/Dockers**....

4.2 Set up the Page

For this new drawing, letter portrait format is not suitable. We therefore want to set the paper format to **Half letter transversely**. This will be in the dialog box, which appears after "new file" as well as at any time in the **Property Bar** (if nothing is marked). We recommend not using the dialog box to change the page format later in the drawing.

- ➢ Start a **new document**.
- ➢ **Turn off** the New Document Window permanently.
  - ✎ You can reactivate every time as follows: **Tools/Options/CorelDraw**, there "**Show New Document**".
- ➢ **If nothing is selected**, the page settings (paper size, etc.) are displayed in the **property bar**.
  - ✎ Click with the pick tool in the empty area, so that nothing is marked.

Select the **paper size** from the list or enter the desired coordinates.

Left: change all pages in this project, **right:** only set the current page.

Select **portrait** or **landscape** format.

Choose the unit e.g. inches or millimetres.

- ➢ You can also set the page size in the **Layout** tab. You should have a look at this menu.
- ♦ For layout, you will also find the **Page Background** command.
  - ✎ In this menu, you can easily select a color or an image as the background of the page.
  - ✎ The bitmap size must be same as page size; if it's smaller, you get tiles.

4.3 Rectangles, Ellipses, Variety

- ➢ Now draw some rectangles and ellipses. The lowest symbol can be used to select the shapes.
- ➢ Save as "**Rectangles and Ellipses**".

Hold down [Ctrl] while drawing to get exact **circles**.

4.4 Marking and Moving

The drawn objects may not fit optimally to the new paper size. No problem:

One object:

- Click on the **Pick Tool** to select it.
  - ↳ The **touch points** appear so that the size can be changed, etc.

Several objects:

- Can be clicked and selected by holding down the [**Shift**] key.
  - ↳ Note the message at the bottom of the **status line**: "X Objects selected...", otherwise it did not work.

Marking frame

- With the selection tool you can drag a large frame, just like a rectangle, except that the selection arrow is a marking frame.
  - ↳ All objects within this frame are highlighted and can now be moved, copied, deleted, and so on.

[Ctrl]-a

- Mark all: [**Ctrl**]-a or **Edit/Select All/Objects** (text, guidelines or nodes an so marked, too).

Exercise: Moving and Resize

- ➤ Select all drawn objects with a **marking frame**,
- ➤ then **move** all at once, either
  - ↳ use the **mouse** to touch a line or
  - ↳ with the **directional buttons**, very precisely, or
  - ↳ specify the new coordinates in the **property bar**.

Change position = move (after Return).

Turn

Mirror: horizontally or vertically.

X: 3,764"   5,81"   100,0 %
Y: 5,197"   4,938" 100,0

Height or width can be modified here, or **scale** with the percentage = increase or decrease.

With the lock activated, both axes are changed simultaneously so that the ratio of height to width is maintained.

Note:

- The **upper row** changes the X-axis, or the width.
- The **lower row** changes the Y-axis or the height.

Notes: ....
....
....
....

4.5 SELECT COLORS

The rectangles are in simple black but somewhat bland. Let us make it colorful. Colors can be selected via the color palette at the right edge of the screen.

- First, mark an object, e.g. a rectangle.
- Then, the color for the selected object can be changed. Just click on a color of the color palette on the right margin.

4.6 THE COLOR PALETTE

Only a few colors are displayed in the visible area of the color palette. The other colors are as follows:

Change to other pallets and various commands.

The / for turned off, means without filling or an invisible frame line.

Turn On color palette

From Black to Grey to White, then follows the other colors.

- If the color palette is turned off:
  - You can activate it again by **Window/Color Palettes**.
  - The default is the "default palette", we'll look at the other palettes below.

With the **left mouse button** as fill color,
Right-click the line color.

Attention! If nothing is selected, you will change the **defaults**. Cancel if warning window appears!

- Assign a **line and fill color** to all drawn elements.
  - In this case, too, you can select several elements with the [Shift] key or with a **marking frame** and assign a color to it at once.

The color palette contains even **more colors**. Use these arrows to move the visible range or

herewith display the **complete color palette**.

At the bottom left, colors already used are displayed and can be assigned to other objects. At the lower right, the fill and line color of the active object is displayed:

C:0 M:100 Y:100 K:0   C:100 M:100 Y:0 K:0 0,567 pt

The **lines** are still very thin. This can also be changed.

4.7 Changing Line Thickness

In order for the outlines to become more visible, we can increase the line thickness with the line icon in the **Property Palette**:

You can also enter any line width here.

None = Without line.

Hairline = very thin line = default setting.

0.5 pt
0.75 pt
1.0 pt
1.5 pt
2.0 pt
3.0 pt
4.0 pt
8.0 pt
10.0 pt
12.0 pt
16.0 pt
24.0 pt
36.0 pt

Here you can choose your preferred line thickness.

Looks different? Use Window-Workspace-Default

- **Window/Dockers/Properties** or **right mouse button** on the object and **Properties** opens all settings.
  - Expand the menu with the small **arrow** if necessary:

➢ Use a large marking frame to select several objects and **change the line thickness**.

➢ Then, change the line and fill colors again.

It could be so colorful:

Do the wheels disappear behind the box? If not, the remedy follows on the next page.

4.8 THE PROPERTY BAR – POSITION

♦ In Corel, what was drawn last is front. If this is filled, everything underneath is hidden. If you have drawn the wheels last, they should be placed behind the car.

    ✎ Instead of marking two wheels, it is easier to mark the car and move it forward.

➤ Right mouse button on the object, then **Order**:

- Move absolutely in front / back.
  - To Front of Page — Ctrl+Home
  - To Back of Page — Ctrl+End
- Layers only necessary for extremely detailed drawings.
  - To Front of Layer — Shift+PgUp
  - To Back of Layer — Shift+PgDn
- One for/back.
  - Forward One — Ctrl+PgUp
  - Back One — Ctrl+PgDn
- In Front Of...
- Behind...
- Reverse Order

When you click an object that is already at the front, all options to set it forward are disabled.

Place the selected object **before or after an object** to be clicked on.

You'll find it in the Menu **Object/Order**, too.

➤ Now select the **polygon**, set it to the front and set a different number of corners.

4.9 UNDO

♦ With the following advice, nothing bad can happen to your project:

    ✎ **Observe** the result on the screen for each action.

    ✎ If the expected has not been entered, select **Undo** immediately.

    ✎ Find the cause (wrong command, not marked, etc.) and find the correct command.

Undo | Redo (=reverse undo).

When you click the triangle, the last actions are listed.

- Forward ...
- Fill
- Duplicate
- Move
- Fill
- Fill
- Modify st...
- Modify st...

In the list, you can select **how far back** you want to remove.

4.9.1 DELETE

Of course, you can also simply delete objects that are not fitting:

➤ Click with the **Pick Tool** on the object to be deleted.

    ✎ Here, too, it is often convenient to select several elements with a selection frame or with the [Shift] key pressed.

➤ When the object is highlighted, which is recognizable by the appearing touch points, press the [Delete] key.

Chapter 5

5. ZOOM AND VIEW

If you expand your frame so that you can see the entire current drawing area well, many mistakes can be avoided from the outset, e.g. non-matching lines.

5.1 ZOOM WITH THE ZOOM TOOL

There are several ways to zoom. The simplest way is as follows:

- Choose the **Zoom Tool** on the left side.
  - You can now use the mouse to zoom:
    left mouse button = zoom in
    right mouse button = zoom out
    or draw a **marking rectangle** by holding down the mouse button.
  - Or use the icons in the **property bar** to zoom in or out (appears when the Zoom Tool is selected):

Increase (+) or decrease (-), are actually unnecessary symbols because the mouse click is enough.

Zoom on marked objects or show **all objects**.

Whole Page with borders or show as big as possible
-in the **Width** or
-in the **Height**.

- With a **Wheel Mouse** you can scroll in/out with the mouse wheel also if the Zoom Tool is not selected and
  - The **panning modus** can start by clicking the wheel.

The Panning modus:

Hold mouse button until the selection window appears:

Zoom   Z
Pan   H

Pan: move the image by pressed mouse button.

Note the following Shortcuts:

- [F3] = zoom out
- [F4] = zoom all objects
- [F9] preview on whole screen, back with [Esc] or mouse click.

5.2 THE ZOOM BUTTON

The Zoom button is also always in the Standard Bar:

For example, with "To Width", the drawing is displayed as wide as possible. "To Selected" appears only if at least one element is marked.

Various zoom levels are available again.

To Fit
To Selected
To Page
To Width
To Height
10%
25%
50%
75%
100%
200%
400%
800%
1600%

F4   **To Fit:** As with [F4], all drawn elements are displayed as large as possible.

5.3 SETTING THE DISPLAY

This information is presented here only because it can cause major problems, e.g. no fillings are displayed. In View, you can choose:

- For **Wireframe**, only outlines, but no fillings are displayed.
  - Previously this was sometimes useful to speed up the image build-up, nowadays in case of accidental switching, a **dangerous option**!
- Usually the display is **Enhanced** (postscript-fillings displayed detailed) or **Normal** (all, but postscript-fillings displayed shadowy).
- **Pixels:** with a higher zoom you see the pixels. But it is not as really printed. So, it uses only as much as the capacity of your computer and graphics card.

Special view options:

- **Simulate Overprints** – with Offset printing it is unfavourable if a bright object is printed over a dark one – this case can be displayed here.
- **Rasterize Complex Effects:** It can help by printing problems if complex effects are output like photos as pixel patterns.

In the View Menu, you will find these interesting functions:

- **Page Sorter View:** Before printing once again, see all pages. To turn it off, select it again or press [Esc].
- **Grid, Rulers, Guidelines:** you can switch it on or off. Just try the grid for now, an explanation follows in the next chapter.
- **Page:** here you can e.g. make the **"Printable Area"** visible. This means the area where your printer can print is, most of the time, a little smaller than the page.
  - **Page Border** displays the set paper size so you can arrange the drawing elements appropriately (default is on).

5.4 SETTINGS OF CORELDRAW

- By **Tools/Options/CorelDraw** you can change the pre-sets of the Corel program,
  - by **Tools/Options/Customization** e.g. you can switch the Command Bars on or off, see next chapter.
- With **Tools/Save Settings as Default** you can save the current drawing settings as a general pre-set.
  - In the appearing menu you can select the desired options to be saved as pre-set.
  - This method also allows you to save the most commonly used paper size, as well as the grid and guideline settings, as the default for all new drawings.

5.5 SWITCH THE COMMAND BARS ON OR OFF

You can also turn on additional toolbars, for example, the Text Toolbar for font settings, or accidentally deactivated toolbars by **Tools/Options/Customization** by the point **Command Bars**.

Overview Command Bars:

- The **Menu Bar** contains File, Edit, View …
- The **Status Bar** shows additional information at the bottom of the Corel window.
- The **Standard Bar** is the most used bar at the top with New File, Open, Save, Print …
- Below is the **Property Bar** with most matching symbols, depending on what is selected.
- **Toolbox**: the command symbols on the left side with the drawing tools.

Exercise Command Bars:

- Turn on deactivated command bars, view them and turn them off again.
  - You can see the effect directly on the screen without having to leave the menu.

The toolbars are initially fixed and cannot be moved. In the **Tools/Options/Customization** Menu you can by **Command Bars** deactivate "Lock toolbars" or on a bar, press the right mouse button (at the edge, not on a symbol).

- **Drag** the **Toolbox** into the drawing and reshape the tool palette at the edges, as soon as the mouse changes to a double arrow.
- **Close** the **Toolbox**. Now turn on the **Toolbox** and push it to the old position (do not release the mouse too early).
  - Finally, click the right mouse button and choose **Look Toolbars** again.

6. Lines

6.1 Freehand Tool

Lines are drawn with the **Freehand Tool**. There are several possibilities. We start with the freehand line.

> ➤ **Freehand Tool:** New drawing on DIN A4 transversely, then select the **Freehand Tool** and press the mouse button to draw:
>
> ➤ The lines are rounded automatically, fewer turning points facilitate subsequent shaping. More about curve processing on page 91.

> If you want to draw a lot of freehand, you should consider the purchase of a **drawing tablet** with a pressure-sensitive pencil, because the mouse is not suitable for freehand drawing. With such a pen the line becomes thicker when you press harder.

> ➤ Complete the drawing by switching to the **Pick Tool** and setting a different color as well as a thicker line.

Not only freehand lines, even straight lines and polygons are possible.

6.1.1 Straight Lines

> ➤ For a **straight line** with the line tool:
>   - First mouse click = **starting point**,
>   - Click elsewhere = **end point**.

6.1.2 Polygon

> ♦ The line tool can be used **to continue** a straight line:
>   - First mouse click = **starting point**, then move the mouse away.
>   - **Double-click** will set a point, but the line continues, so you can add with double-click as many lines as you want.
>   - Until you set the **end point** with one click.
>
> ➤ Draw a triangle or a carnival cap!

LINDEMANN B/H/IT © DIPL.-ING. (FH) PETER SCHIESSL

6.2 Lines in an Angle

Horizontal or vertical lines or lines at the following angles: 15°, 30°, 45°, 60°, 90° etc. can be drawn in this easy way:

➤ Set the **start point** as usual, move the mouse away, and hold down the [Ctrl] key.

  ✏ If you rotate the mouse pointer around the starting point, you can see that the line is drawn only at these angles.

➤ Drag a **horizontal line** across the entire page:

6.3 Exercise Lines

➤ Draw the following in your drawing, then save as "lines and shapes":

Click the start point once - double-click - double-click - click the end point once. After drawing, try to apply the figures and filling color.

To fill items, the line must be closed, meaning the end point must be exactly on the start point.

6.4 Exercise Convertible

➤ New drawing on DIN A5 transversally and **save as convertible**.

➤ Draw a horizontal line as a road, draw a wheel as a circle (hold down the [Ctrl] key), set a thick line for the tire, and a matching fill color.

➤ **Copy** this circle when finished, for the second wheel, and also arrange it above the road line.

➤ Draw the chassis out of closed lines (double-click), then select a Fill Color and move backwards (right mouse button – order, or [Ctrl]-Page down) so that the wheels are in front. **The symbols in the property bar disappear if more than one object is selected.**

[Ctrl]-Page up/down

➤ Finally, draw the front disc as a triangle of lines, fill and set to the body of the car.

6.5 Pencil Types

If you hold the mouse on the freehand pin tool, you can switch to additional line types in the menu that appears:

- Freehand — F5 — The **normal line** used so far.
- 2-Point Line — Line also possible as **tangent**:
- Bézier — **Curves** (press and move the mouse).
- Pen — **Pen**: lines from click to click in combination with curves (press and move the mouse for curves).
- B-Spline — **B-Spline**: define curves through clicks, stop with a double-click.
- Polyline — **Polyline**: Line from click to click, stop with double-click.
- 3-Point Curve

Instead the "Bezier, B-Spline, 3-Point-Curve" curves are easier to create and adjust with curve processing. See details on page 91. So, in this menu only the Freehand line and the Polyline are recommended.

6.6 Artistic Media Tools

Below the pen is the **Artistic Media Tool** with a variety of fascinating and interesting drawing features.

➤ Start a new drawing and choose the **Artistic Media Tool**. In the **Property Bar** you will now find the following setting options:

The Pen-Types:
- Pre-set
- Brush
- Sprayer
- Calligraphic

Descriptions follow.

Select a pre-set shape.

The **thickness**.

Automatic **smoothing**.

You can only use the pressure sensitive pen if you have an appropriate drawing tablet.

Select pencil type and shape, then paint. However, you can also **change** the shape after the object is selected or even assign the shapes to other drawn elements. For example, mark a rectangle, then select a preset line shape or an image spray can. With **Effects/Artistic Media**, you will find these pen types again as docking windows.

6.6.1 Artistic Media Tools - Preset

Instead of a line of uniform width, you can select specific line shapes, e.g. a wedge-shaped line or a water droplet.

6.6.2 ARTISTIC MEDIA TOOLS - BRUSH

These brushes paint beautiful wallpaper patterns on the page.

Note the type selection list.

First, choose a type, then a form.

6.6.3 ARTISTIC MEDIA TOOLS - SPRAYER

With the Sprayer you can **spray a series of images** with the mouse button pressed down. Try some types using the two selection buttons:

6.6.4 ARTISTIC MEDIA TOOLS - CALLIGRAPHIC

If you paint sideways with a wide brush, the line is quite thin, but crosswise wide. This gives the calligraphic effects (e.g. when painting Chinese or Japanese characters). You can simulate such brush strokes with this function, whereby the width of the brush and the rotation can be specified.

➢ Draw a Japanese letter, first increase the angle for a flat brush to 60 °.

6.7 Exercise Pen

- Paint with the **Pen Tool** the boat (straight lines), two rectangles for the blue sky and the darker water (fill blue), head and body as ellipses, and hair with the pen.
- The rest (clouds, balloons, waves, hair, ...) are brush or sprayer effects.

Sprayer for clouds and balloons.

Waves with the brush.

Two filled rectangles, light blue for the sky, dark blue for the water.

Try it and you see how easy it is and realize your own ideas!

6.8 Smart Fill Tool

The Smart Fill Tool allows you to fill in intersections:

- Draw a rectangle and circle and try it out.

Switch here to the **Smart Fill Tool**, specify the filling and line color in the Property Bar - and click on the cut section. Works only with unfilled objects!

6.9 Smart Drawing

By the Artistic Media Tools, you can select the Smart Drawing Tool:

[Shift]-S

If the Smart Drawing Tool is activated, you can draw with a pressed left mouse button and Corel will try to complete and close a form (rectangle, circle, polygon...). Try it:

6.10 Live Scetch

S

This tool is a very smooth pen. Try drawing with it an apple or a car. Don't forget to close the molds, i.e. End point to the start point if the objects are to be filled.

Second Part

Precise Drawing

Square, Circle, Grid, Guidelines, Text, Group

7. PRECISE DRAWING

7.1 THE GRID

The Grid is a useful aid in precise drawing.

- For example, if the **Grid** is activated, aligned, and set to a distance of 5 mm, all newly drawn parts are arranged on this 5 mm grid.
  - Crawling measures, such as a line from start point 45,05756 / 33,45666, are thus avoided from the outset and can be accurately drawn without any effort.

The grid can be set up most easy in this way: **Right mouse button on the ruler, then "Grid Setup...":**

Always switch to **inches apart** (description follows)!

Whether you want to see the grid is a matter of taste, but aligning with the grid should be activated in any case, except when drawing freehand.

More with the grid:

- With **View/Grid** you can show or hide the grid points,

[Ctrl]-Y

- With **View/Snap to** you can activate or deactivate the alignment of the various grids or guidelines.
  - **Baseline Grid**: Horizontal help lines similar to lined paper are displayed in the set point distance.
  - **Guidelines**: Sometimes, it is not enough to draw help lines into the drawing. Only when by View activated "Snap to guidelines", new drawings aligned with help lines.

Notes on the grid:

- **4 grid lines per inch** = grid points every 0.25 **inches**,
  10 grid lines per inch = grid points every 0.1 **inches**.
- The grid points are automatically displayed with some space between.
  - If the view is very reduced, Corel removes the grid points so that a black drawing full of grid points is not displayed.

7.1.1 EXERCISE: PYRAMIDS FROM SQUARES

Draw the following pyramid from squares.

> ➢ New drawing, Half Letter crosswise, adjust the grid to a distance of 0.2 inch.

[Ctrl]

> ➢ Then draw a **square** (hold down [Ctrl] key or use the grid) and **copy** multiple times using the mouse:
>
> > ✎ **Move** and click the **right mouse button** on the way, and release the left button at the destination.
>
> ♦ When drawing, moving, and reshaping, note whether the cursor jumps to the grid points (if necessary, touch the corner).
>
> > ✎ If not, check to see if the grid is activated, the distance is correct, and the Alignment is set to On.

Handling at the **corner** helps to move so as to fit the grid.

Mark a row with the Pick Tool and a larger border, then fill the squares with **color**.

> While holding down the [Ctrl] key, you can draw squares instead of rectangles, circles instead of ellipses, and lines at these angles: 0 °, 15 °, 30 °, 45 °, 60 °, 90 °, etc.

> ➢ Save this exercise as "pyramid squares", as this is reused later.

7.1.2 FURTHER ON THE GRID

Now we've set up the grid and can draw with it exactly. At least the good expression makes the change hardly noticeable.

♦ If you draw a **detail greatly enlarged,** you can fine-tune the grid, by every millimetre or even every 0.1 mm.

♦ The grid is optimal and should **always be used**, so that everything fits effortlessly. The only exceptions are genuine freehand drawings, with [Alt]-Y, temporarily switch off the grid feature.

[Alt]-Y

7.2 Copy and Move

[Ctrl]-D

- You can also create a copy using the **Edit/Duplicate** command.
- If the **Pick Tool** is active a selected Element can be moved precisely with the directional buttons in the property bar.
  - ↳ But if no object is selected (if necessary, click with the Pick Tool in an empty area), the **step size** and **duplicate distance** can be set there:

The step width when moving with the directional buttons can be adjusted at any time - Practical for precise and easy moving.

Space between **duplicates**.

The default setting:

> You can specify the step size in the property bar, or in the menu with **double click on the ruler**.
> ↳ For example, at 0.01", you can move the elements marked with the direction buttons by 0.01" each. The larger step size applies when the [Shift] key is pressed, e.g. you could specify 10 for 10x0.01" here.

It is best to overwrite it with suitable values like your preferences and save it as a default.

The smaller step width by pressing the [Ctrl] key. Try 5.0, super nude 10 and micro nude 5 and save it as a preset.

Exercise:

> Create rectangles and lines using copy, then rotate and move them to make the following farm. Make the work easier by **increasing** as much as you draw.

Draw once, copy often.

7.3 Guidelines Setup

The question remains: how are objects easier to arrange at the same height, e.g. the windows of the previous exercise? With the **guidelines**.

Important notes about the guidelines:

- Guidelines are not printed, but the objects can be aligned exactly on these lines. Guidelines are therefore optimal to specify page margins or to arrange elements flush.
- **Rulers/Grid/Guidelines** visible/invisible and adjust the alignment:

7.3.1 Set Guidelines and Move

The **rulers** are located at the top and left from the drawing area:

- Pull with the left mouse button from the ruler into the drawing - a guideline is there.
  - Pulling from the horizontal **Ruler** you can pull horizontal guidelines into the drawing.
  - Pulling from the vertical **Ruler** you can pull vertical guidelines into the drawing.
- **Delete Guidelines**: click on the guideline and press [Del].

Exercise:

- Start a new drawing, again DIN A5-cross.
- **First, align your grid with lines every 5mm.**
  - If you now draw guidelines into the drawing, **they will also be aligned to the grid** as long as you release the mouse near a grid point (note the appearing marks).
- Then drag two horizontal and two vertical guides as a **side-edge** into the drawing.

Move Guidelines:

- Try to **move** a vertical and a horizontal help line: click and drag them to another location.

Now we turn a Guideline:

- Pull another guideline in the middle of it. When clicking on it, the arrows on which the guideline can be **rotated** appear outside.
  - You can also specify the **angle of rotation** in the property bar (confirm with Return). Right of the angle you can set the center of rotation.
- The **guideline menu** is useful when many help lines are set:
  - To open the menu, double click on a guideline or
  - **Right mouse button** on the Ruler, then "**Guidelines Setup**".

7.3.2 THE GUIDELINES-MENU

By double clicking on a guideline you can open the menu divided into horizontal, vertical and all guidelines:

Guidelines **visible** or invisible.

Important: Snap to guidelines.

Line type and color for highlighted guidelines.

Here you can enter **precise coordinates** and set with **Add**, respectively for horizontal, vertical or angled-guidelines. If you click on a guideline below, you can also change it here, e.g. correct from crooked coordinates 4.248 to the even value 4.25.

In the menu above you will find these symbols at the bottom:

Delete the actual marked guideline (or with [Del] also.

Lock Guideline: Then the guidelines cannot be moved or deleted.

7.3.3 ANGLED GUIDELINES-MENU

Here you can define angles for existing guidelines or set new guidelines in an angle:

Switch in the Guidelines-Menu to the angled-guidelines.

Enter the coordinates and the **angle**, and you can set guidelines with the exact desired angle by clicking on "Add" (possible to move later in the drawing).

If a guideline is marked, you'll find in the **Property Bar** this symbol with pre-sets e.g. for one cm margins and more.

When you first set up the **grid**, guidelines are pulled into the drawing as desired.

7.4 ALIGNING ON

The help lines are not used as long as the objects are not aligned with them.

[Alt]-Y
- With **View** you can switch on/off the visibility of the Grid or Guidelines.
- With **View/Snap To** you can switch on/off the snap function of the Grid or Guidelines.

Activated Functions marked with the: ✓.

- **Dynamic guidelines** make constructing easier, since they appear automatically and indicate angles or references.

In the **Property Bar** you can directly set if a guideline is marked:

lock / snap on / menu on or off / pre-sets.

7.5 EXERCISE: TRUCK

➢ Start a new drawing **crosswise** and save as "Truck".
➢ Also possible: Page setup: **6 x 3 meters** and **Grid** each **0.2 m**.
➢ Set below a horizontal line as the street.

So it should be:

Closed and filled freehand line.

Colored rectangles only!

To fill the load: continue to the starting point, select fill color and set backwards.

Thick black outline for the tire and a single-colored filling as a rim.

The Wheels:

➢ Draw the wheels as **circles** by pressing [Ctrl] or using the grid so it doesn't become a ellipse.
➢ Copy the first **wheel** twice. If you press [Shift] by copying you can move them exactly horizontally.

8. Quadrates, Circles, Shapes

8.1 Quadrates and Circles

We have already created squares and circles by pressing the [Ctrl] key in the truck exercise before.

- By pressing **[Ctrl]-Left Mouse Button** you can draw
  - **Lines** in 15°-degree steps including 45°, 90° etc.
  - Instead of an **ellipse**, it will draw a **circle** and
  - instead of a **rectangle**, a **quadrate**.

> [Ctrl] = Circle, Quadrate; exact angle.

- While pressing **[Shift]-Left Mouse Button**
  - a started ellipse, circle or rectangle **will be drawn around the first point** (the first point is the middle point and not the edge point as usual) or
  - you can change the size of objects around their middle point or
  - with **[Ctrl]+[Shift]** together you can draw a circle or quadrate around the first point.

> [Shift]= around first point.

- Usage: This way, you can **draw a circle exactly around a point** or axis intersection point. If you click on this point and start drawing your object, you can press and hold [Ctrl]+[Shift] while drawing.

You do not have to remember this, just try it:

- Draw an ellipse or rectangle, but keep the **left mouse button pressed** and then **try**:
  - [Ctrl] or [Shift]-Button or both?
  - You'll see the effect on the screen as soon as you move the mouse slightly!

> **Press and hold the left mouse button and try!**
>
> If you want to move elements with the left mouse button pressed, or copy them with an additional right-click, it helps to touch the corner so that they remain on the grid points.

8.1.1 Exercise: Quadrates and Circles with Guidelines and Grid

➤ New Drawing with letter crosswise, save as "Quadrates and Circles".

➤ Draw for the exact horizontal arrangement with a guideline (and activate "Snap to Guidelines" first):

➤ For this **new drawing** use the **grid every 0.2"** and draw one quadrate, then copy it with right mouse button. With one line or some quadrates ready, you can mark and copy multiple objects at once:

Now comes a very difficult but useful exercise:

➤ The differently colored filling is produced by copying the outer, largest circle several times inwards.

   ↳ Hold down the **[Shift]** key so that the copied circles automatically get the same middle point.

➤ Fill each copied circle with the desired **color**.

[Shift] = Reduce or enlarge around the center point.

Draw the outer circle, then touch and reduce the touch point at the corner.
Click the **right mouse** button to initiate copying, and then hold the [Shift] key to decrease the center point.

This is no problem if you press the **right mouse button** during the movement + holding down the left mouse button, then you can at any time try pressing [Shift] or [Ctrl] to find the target position.

8.2 Polygon, Spiral, Grinding

Corel also offers special shapes, which can be found with the polygon tool under the symbols for rectangles and circles. Draw the following:

Draw first with the default, then you can set each of these elements by mouse or in the **property bar**. Thus, e.g. triangles (=three corners), octagons or stars:

Mirroring, horizontal or vertical.

How many corners should the star or polygon have?

At these points, the polygon can be shaped by means of the **Shape Tool** by mouse.

8.3 Common Shapes: Basic, Arrow, Flowchart etc.

Corel also has prefabricated standard shapes, e.g. for a flash, an arrow or various stars or speech bubbles.

> In the **polygon menu**, see above, you will find the **Common Shapes** (Basic, Arrow Flowchart etc.), too. Select a form type, then you can select more in the **property bar**, here a sample for the Arrow Shapes:

Select a group in the **Polygon** menu, then the desired shape type in the **property bar**.

Of course, these shapes can also be **retrofitted**. Note the tap points.

9. Ruler, Zero Point, Group

It is sometimes helpful to lay the **zero point** appropriately, for one wheel, for example, in the centre. Or to adjust the **scale** from the start instead, to manually count every dimension later.

9.1 Ruler and Zero Point

In order to specify the dimensions for a drawing, a **Zero point** is set and is scaled up horizontally (X-axis) and vertically (Y-axis).

In a CorelDRAW Drawing you can read the coordinates on the **rulers** at the top and left of the screen and usually the zero point is the left bottom of the page, but depending on the drawing the zero point is sometimes better placed in the middle with 0 or lower right.

(0, 0)

Move the zero point: Use the mouse to move the zero point to a new position from this symbol. It is recommended to activate the **Grid** first.

The **zero point** is by default at the lower end of the page. From there, counting is carried out in the positive and negative directions, so that a point with the coordinates is specified, e.g. 40/85.

- ♦ Double-clicking on the ruler displays the settings menu.
   - ✏ In this menu, you could **change the unit** for the ruler to meters or inches, or **specify the start position** (0,0) at origin.
   - ✏ e.g. if you enter with a paper sized DIN A5 crosswise horizontal 210 is the zero point on the right side of paper.

If you click on the menu item **"Edit Scale"**, a window appears, in which you can choose other scales:

Choose a scale above or set it manually, e.g. for a map 1" **Page distance** corresponds to 1000" World distance.

9.2 Exercise: Railway Wheel

We want to draw a railway wheel. Preparations:

➢ Start a new drawing, choose centimetres as the units and set the size to 100x100 cm:

➢ Double-click on the ruler and set the **origin at 50, 50 cm** so that it is exactly in the center of the page.

  ↳ Then, use the **Zoom Tool** to select "Whole Page" to see the result.

➢ Place the **grid every 5 cm** (centimetres apart) and turn on the grid and guidelines.

> Attention! Corel only points at the grid points when you click or release near a point!

➢ Set a horizontal **Guideline** at 0 and a vertical at 0 because the origin 0/0 is now in the center of the page.

Drawing is easier now with the guidelines and grid:

➢ Draw a large circle: Set the starting point exactly in the middle, then draw the circle while pressing **[Ctrl]+[Shift]-Button** around this middle point.

➢ We cannot simply draw the smaller circle, since we could move the first circle. Therefore, we copy the first circle and reduce it:

  ↳ Touch and hold down the corner handles, right-click for copying, press [Shift], locate the target position and release the mouse.

  ↳ Mark both circles, then **combine** them and choose a filling color.

➢ Just as the **small axis circles** can be drawn, combining would not be necessary here since both circles can be filled simply in color if the smaller circle is at the front.

➢ Now draw the first horizontal spoke and place it at the back. If necessary, switch off the grid using [Ctrl]-Y.

The first spoke is copied while rotating:

① When you click the first spoke twice, the arrows and the pivot point appear.

Copy this combined circle out again and fill it brighter.

② Pull the **pivot point** before turning to the center of the circles.

③ Hold on to one of the arrows and press [Ctrl] to copy it several times (right mouse click).

9.3 The Menu "Transform"

Actions with the mouse go quickly, but those elements can be inadvertently moved just as quickly. If you want to be more precise, you can use the Transformation Menu Window/Dockers/Transform.

[Alt]-F7

You can use the different map types to perform all actions as with the mouse, except that you enter exact coordinates here. This offers two advantages:

- It is more comfortable and you can undo all actions here, even after you have executed numerous other commands.
  An example:
  - It can be drawn without accidentally moving a **background** - it can temporarily be moved by 300 mm to the side edge - when everything is done, the background is reset by -300 mm.

Perfectly draw the railway wheel:

> Use the **Undo** to erase the rotated spokes from the exercise using the mouse, then rotate the first spoke (the centre of rotation is already in the centre of the wheel) with the **Transform-Menu**.
>> If the **angle of rotation** does not fit evenly, reverse and try again with a different angle.

Add rivets:

The rotation works so well that we can rotate same way some rivets

> Draw with a high zoom **one rivet as a radial filled circle.**

> Move the rotation point in the middle and **copy** around the wheel:

Draw **one rivet as a radial filled circle** and **copy** it the same way as the spokes with **Transform-Menu** around the wheel.

> Afterwards, mark all with a big selection frame or [Ctrl]-A and **Group Objects**.

> **Save** as "railway wheel" because we'll need it later to copy into our drawing of the train.

9.4 GROUP OBJECTS

Complex drawings are not a problem if they are divided into small groups. As soon as a wheel is finished, for example, this can be grouped into one element and can then be duplicated as often as required.

Advantages of Grouping:

- Easy to **copy** or move because only one object needs to be selected.
- There is no more danger of **inadvertently moving** or deleting a small part like a rivet while you continue tracing.

Different ways of Grouping:

- You can group by symbol in the property bar (far right), in the menu (Object/Group...) or with the shortcut **[Ctrl]-G**.
   - ↳ Grouping is only possible if several elements have been selected.
   - ↳ If "**Ungroup**" is active instead of Grouping, the actual marked has already been grouped.

Group makes from several elements one group by conserving their individual attributes.

Combine makes one Object so you can fill it with color.

If you want to edit an element of a group again:

- While holding down the [Ctrl] key, single elements can be selected from a group and edited individually.
   - ↳ For example, to assign a different color, you must release the [Ctrl] key to pick the color.
- Or you could **un-group**, edit items as usual, and then re-group them. The latter is recommended for extensive modifications.

9.4.1 EXERCISE: BLOSSOM

We'll do a similar exercise to the railway wheel, but this one may be easier.

- ➢ We want to draw a blossom: new drawing, draw a **circle** in the middle and one **ellipse** as the first petal.
- ➢ **Rotate** the ellipse like petals around the flower. Before turning, push the **center of rotation** into the middle.
- ➢ Then, **mark** and group everything with a large selection frame or [Ctrl]-A.
- ➢ While holding down the [Ctrl] key, select individual petals from the group and change the color.

The circle in the middle was set to the back.

Chapter 10

10. TEXT AND SYMBOLS

10.1 TEXT EDITING IN COREL

➢ Start a new drawing A4 crosswise, then choose the text-editing tool (A).

Now you have to tell the computer where you want to place the text., because we are using a drawing program, not a text program, and can put the text anywhere.

➢ Click on the desired location in the drawing and write: "Sample Text"

➢ **Copy this sample text sometimes** as training material. You can copy text similar to other objects this way:

★ Use the **Pick Tool** to move, and then **copy** it multiple times using the **right mouse button**.

10.1.1 TEXT FORMATTING WITH THE PROPERTY BAR

The easiest way to format the text, as in a word processor, is with the **Property Bar**.

➢ When you click a text, you will find these icons for text formatting in the feature bar:

- Angle of Rotation
- Horizontal Alignment: Without, **Left**, Center, Full Justify, Force Justify (Last line is also stretched to the right edge).
- Font Type
- Font Size
- Bold, italic, underlined.
- Edit text: a text window opens. Useful for text sometimes distorted with effects.
- Text Formatting: a menu opens with many options.

Looks different? Use Window-Workspace-Default

♦ Select what you want to adjust:

✎ by pressing the [**Shift**] key with the **Pick Tool**,

✎ Or by pressing the left mouse button within a text with the **Text Tool**.

10.1.2 MODIFY TEXT WITH THE PICK TOOL

When you finish the text editing, the **text is an object** like a rectangle or line, so you can edit the text as well:

- Click on the text with the Pick Tool once:
  - to change the **text size at the Handle Points** or
  - to catch the text and move it to another position (try to click on the text body, not on a handle point) or
  - Click while moving the right mouse button for copying.
- Click on the text with the Pick Tool a second time and you can:

| With the middle arrows, make customized *italic* text. |
| The rotation point can also be moved with the mouse. |
| Turn the text with the corner arrows. |

Sample Text

That's how it should be:

Sample Text

Also note by text the difference between lines and fill color.

Move the **turn middle point** left from the text, then copy with the menu with Window/Dockers/Transform or by pressing the [Ctrl] key in exactly **30 degrees**. Last **group** the text spiral to one object.

Double clicking on text switches to the Text Tool!

10.2 Exercise: Solar

To complete the basics for drawing, let's try an exercise with lines, a circle and text. Draw the following **letterhead** before setting up grids and guide lines:

Preparation:

- New Drawing, *set page with* 80x50mm or if you prefer inch 30"x20", set **Grid** suitable, two **Guidelines** and activate **Snap On**.

Circle and Lines:

- Draw the **Circle** ([Ctrl] key) for the sun with yellow filling and line.
- Draw the first vertical **line**:
  - Click two times on this line (not a double-click) and move the **center point** to the center of the sun.
  - Now you can copy each turn with right mouse button click and press the **[Ctrl]** key on the lines each 15°.
- Draw the rectangle for the solar module and rotate and arrange it appropriately to shorten the solar beams.

Corner Rounding:

- For the rounding of the corners, you can find these controls in the Properties bar:

The corners can be set manually using the **Shape Tool**.

When the lock is closed, all four corners are coupled.

- Write the **text** and format it centered, place two rectangles as a background and fill it appropriately.
  - Use the **grid or the coordinate fields** in the property bar to set the rectangles to **exact coordinates** so you can place the text perfectly in the middle of it.
- Mark all with **[Ctrl]-A** or a big mark rectangle and group it – so it is useable as **letterhead**. .
  - Copy it into your **word processing program** as letterhead in the header. You can export in CorelDRAW as a **wmf file** for the best compatibility with MS Office programs.

10.3 THE SYMBOL FONTS

The content of Windows and the Corel program package are special fonts that contain pictures instead of letters. Of these fonts only examples were installed on your computer, as every installed font occupy memory.

- New exercise: the **menu for symbol fonts** can be opened with **[Ctrl]-[F11]** or Text/Glyphs.

On the right side, a docker appears:

With these arrows ▶▶ the toolbar can be displayed or hidden, with the **X** you can switch off the docker.

Choose the font here.
It is recommended to browse through the pages for the first time to check which fonts are available (note Webdings and Wingdings),

then pull the desired symbol with the mouse into the drawing

or click on the symbol, **copy** it and then click with the Text Tool in the drawing – you can choose a position in an existing text, too – and insert.

Notice the scroll bar on the right for even more selection.

Interesting fonts: **Yu Gothic** and **MS Reference Speciality** with fractions and special characters, **Wingdings, Webdings, Symbol,** fonts with Chinese characters: **MingLiU** and **MS JhengHei**.

Integrate a symbol into a text:

These special characters can also be inserted into a text from this Corel menu: if the text is opened with the text tool (cursor flashes at the desired location), double-click on the character you want to insert.

Then, the special character is inserted into the text, consequently just as a normal letter moves and changes e.g. with the font size.

Only the font can't be changed afterwards because the new font also applies to the special character. If it is necessary to change the font type of the text, then reinsert the symbol or reassign the character font to the symbol.

After inserting the object correctly with the **Shape Tool** the letter distance should match up.

Third Part

Colors

Fillings, ClipArt, Photos

Basics Color Models:

- ◆ CMYK: the color model used by offset printing and every four color printer. It means: C=CYAN, M=MAGENTA, Y=YELLOW, K=BLAC<u>K</u>.
- ◆ RGB is the color sheme of every monitor and TV. All colors are mixed from the base colors <u>R</u>ED, <u>G</u>REEN and <u>B</u>LUE.
  - ✎ RGB is a so named **additive color scheme**, because all colors together result in white (light is mixed), while by CMYK all colors together result in black, all colors off in white (= **subtractive scheme**).

11. Single Fillings

11.1 Overview select Filling and adjust

- You can choose colors from the **color palette**:
  - Select the object and change the **fill color** with the left mouse button, and the **line color** with the right one.
- For more precise color selection or special color fillings, there are two options by this symbol in the **Tool Bar**:

Interactive Fill tool: use the Edit Fill symbol in the Property Bar, or use the mouse to adjust the object.

Smart Fill tool: set fill and line color in the Property Bar and click on object to fill. Smart because recognize **intersections**.

Filling of a intersection.

A detailed description of both methods follows.

11.2 Modify the Preset

Before we set colors, a little hint. If **nothing is selected**, Corel assumes that you want to change the **general preferences**. Two examples to illustrate this:

- If **nothing is selected** and you click a **color**, you could set this color as the default for all new objects.

- If **nothing is selected** and you select a line **thickness** from the line menu (pencil symbol), all lines will be drawn with this thickness in the future.

- This can be arbitrarily extended, e.g. If you select a different **font** without a text selected, you could save this font as a default.

Therefore, for each action: if **nothing is selected**, you change the default setting if you confirm the appearing **warning window** with OK:

You **cannot undo** this! You can only reset it by the reverse process, e.g. select without something marked to make the line color black, or no fill color.

Usually, if this window appears accidentally, then **Cancel**.

If you change the default settings with **OK**, this applies only to the current drawing. By **Tools/Save Settings as Default** you can also save the presets for all new drawings.

11.3 The Color Palette

- Open the **Pyramid Squares exercise** so you can try something out.
- **Open** some more color palettes by **Window/Color Palettes/Palettes**, under Process and Spot the interesting pallets can be found.
- **Close** all open palettes but not the Default palette. You can close unmark by **Window/Color Palettes/Palettes** or by this arrow at top of the pallet:

Close a palette by this arrow and then **Palette-Close**.

If you want to select many colors, it is convenient to drag the **color palette** into the center of the drawing.

So colors can choose easy:

Hold at these points and pull them to the centre, then adjust the window size at the edges or corners.

Back: pull at the top of the bar, and drag with the mouse to the right edge of the window until the color-coded position frame appears. Easier, if you **close all dockers windows before**.

- You can switch to a different color palette by **Window/Color Palettes**, which is automatically positioned right again.

  ↳ By **Window/Color Palettes** you can **switch off** color palettes.

Instead of using the palettes, you can also adjust each color manually.

11.4 COLOR SETTINGS

You can also choose a color as you like on this way:

Edit Fill

Uniform Fill

○ Color viewers   ○ Color palettes

HSB - Hue Based

Color area or color palettes – see next page.

Color model: CMYK

Name:

R: 225
G: 114
B: 39

#E17227

H: 24
S: 82
B: 88

Preselect the color with the slider below, then set the color point in the color area.

old color / new color / swap with the arrows.

Pick up a color from your desktop.

11.5 Color Palettes

CorelDRAW has some color palettes. Switch to the palettes in the previous menu:

*Switch here to the **Palettes**, e.g. Process/Pantone/Pantone+.*

"Show color name": So you can tell the printery the color numbers and all colors are printed correct.

Here you find the color number, too.

About the Palettes:

- **Palettes** are standardized color catalogues used by **painters and printers**, so that colors can be accurately reproduced, e.g.:
- Colors according to the **Focoltone**, a scheme you use when you paint your rawhide wallpaper.
- **Pantone** colors are the standard in graphics and printing, and are also used for interior decoration, cosmetics and product design.
- The printers and painters have **catalogs** of these color palettes and can thus reproduce exactly the desired color.
- By **Window/Color Palettes** you find all commands for color palettes, here you could also create your own palette.

The palettes are very important when a color needs to be exactly reproduced:

- If you change the painter or the printing company, the stationery letterhead or the business card can be printed again in exactly the same colors.
  - If you use the palette colors in Corel and specify the numbers to the printer, the colors fit as planned.
  - It is ideal if you use a **printed color palette catalogue** because your monitor and printer don't show the colors exactly the same.

> The use of the color palettes allows identical colors on business cards, letterheads, company signs, painting, etc. Depending on your version, CorelDRAW does not have all or other palettes available.

Chapter 12

12. Fountain Fill

Color Gradient Fillings are nice and versatile.

➢ Open the exercise "**Pyramids Squares**" (s. P. 44) and choose the "**Interactive Fill Tool**".

Now we choose the next option, "Fountain Fill":

- X = shut off filling,
- **Uniform fill**,
- **Fountain Fill**, e.g. color transition from orange to green,
- **Vector pattern fill**: Brick wall, chessboard, coins, stones…,
- **Bitmap pattern fill**: Cherries, tablets, peanuts…,
- **Two color pattern fill**: easy fillings with only two colors,
- **Texture fill** and **PostScript fill**.

Click on the color point, then select a color from the color button.

Use the slider to move the color center point.

In these next exercises, you can try various filling types in each square:

Exercise Pyramids Squares

Text can fill, too.

LINDEMANN B/H/IT © DIPL.-ING. (FH) PETER SCHIESSL

12.1 Adjust the Fountain Fill

You can change a fill at any time. Let's try it. The fountain fill should be at the -37° angle.

➢ Choose the **Interactive Fill Tool**, then click on a new rectangle and **edit the fill** in the property bar on the right-most symbol:

The interactive fill could be adjusted with the mouse, in the Property bar or here you can open the **menu with all the options for fillings**.

Here in the menu you can easily set up the filling:

The alignment: linear, elliptical, conical, rectangular. Please try!

Various, very interesting presets.

Here it is possible to select the direction in which Corel passes through the color disk to get from the initial color to the end color. Different intermediate tones are the result.

Select the start and end color: Click on the color point and then select a color by the color button.

Here you can set the angle. This also allows for a horizontal color profile, too.

The alignment:

linear:	elliptical:	conical	rectangular:

➢ Try different fountain fillings and set them to some squares of the exercise.

12.2 Multiple Color Filling

With these settings for the color profile, a two-color or multi-color filling can also be achieved.

Set up the color gradient filling:

The direction through the color disk = different gradient colors are the result.

Double-click in the bar to set additional color points, then select a color for the new color point. You can move every color point with the mouse. Double-click again to delete a color point.

- The **initial and final colors** can also be selected on the square boxes at the left and right end of the bar.
- Any number of additional color points can be set. For each point a color can be determined.
- Color points can be moved with the mouse.

The **preset 256 color streaks** cause smooth transitions, since the fine stripes are not visible. Multi-strips cause unnecessary computational overhead, but sometimes it is desirable to deliberately reduce the number of strips so that the individual color strips become visible, e.g. to draw a flag.

- To change the number of strips, the checkmark is to be set. Then try to reduce it from 256 to e.g. 90, 9 or 3.
- By **Transformations**, the size of the color gradient can be set, at 80% the 20% at the edge remains with the start and end color.

- If you have a **border area** in this area:
    - **Default:** the start and end color
    - **Repeat & Mirror:** the fountain fill starts again, mirrored.
    - **Reverse:** the fountain fill starts again from the start to end color.

Default	Repeat & Mirror	Reverse

12.3 Exercise: Christmas Card

An easy exercise with many color gradient fillings:

> Use the format **Japanese Postcard crosswise**:

Polygon-Banner shapes.

Draw a tree with the polyline (by pen):

> With the **Polyline,** click once for the next line, Double-Click to stop. Draw roughly from the end to the starting point.

> Then, choose the **Shape Tool** and correctly move the points until it becomes like a Christmas tree.

> Finally, set a green fill.

The tree trunk and the jewelry:

- Paint the **trunk** (freehand line) with a brown filling, then set **backwards** - so you can draw the trunk higher and so the section does not match exactly.
- Finally draw the **jewelry** as filled circles once, then copy several times. Ideal: radial or rectangular color filling or a preset.

> Draw with **Freehand Line**: double-click draws further, one click stops or as **Polyline:** single click draws further, double-click stops.

Group and duplicate the Christmas tree:

- **Mark** the tree with a bigger mark rectangle using the **Pick Tool** and **group it** (with symbol or Object/Group).
  - Now as a group you can easily copy the tree by clicking the right mouse button while moving it to another side.

The Gifts:

- Draw the **gifts**, each with a different fill and line color as filled rectangles.
- Place the gifts **forward or backward** accordingly. Finally, group the gifts.
- We have used a basic form. It would be nicer if you searched in Corel Connect or the web for a clipart.

Text and background:

- Write the **Text** as usual with the **Text tool** and move it to the right position with the mouse. For an exact position you can use the coordinate fields in the Property bar,
- Set a rectangle with fountain fill and rounded edges behind the text on the top,
- Use the **Polygon tool** and find the **Banner shapes**.
- Use it to draw a **big rectangle** with same dimensions as the paper, set it in the background, and format it with a fountain fill.

12.4 Exercise: Carton home

Create a template for a door sign.

Prepare drawing:

- New file, page format **DIN A5 high**. Set a **grid width of 5mm** and align to grid.
- Set guidelines as edge boundaries.

Copy the rectangles:

- Draw the **first rectangle** and adjust it in size.
- Complete the first row by copying. If necessary, delete it again and change the size of the first rectangle.
- Make a **group** out of the first line, then copy this line twice downward.
- Make a **group** of the first block again and copy a second time downward right.

- Mark all and set a matching fountain fill with an angle (see next page).
  - Aslant fountain fills are very nice most of the time but the direction should be not right down, but top right.
- Complete the **text**, write **"Carton-"**, click elsewhere, and write **"home"**, click on another place and write **"Manufacture"**.
- Now you can set these three graphic texts to the guideline on the left side and expand to the guideline on the right side. At last, expand it above to set the height.
  - If finished, mark the text and set a matching **fountain fill**.
- Complete it with the address block left bottom. Copy the filling.
- Mark all text and add a **Drop Shadow** and choose in the Property bar the preset **Medium Glow**. In the Property bar you can choose a nice **color** for the shadow:

> Finish the exercise with a rectangle the same size as the paper and a fountain fill as the background. Here we use a **conical-reverse fountain fill**:

12.5 Exercise: Steam Locomotive

This drawing is already challenging in a course with support, but it is a good exercise that shows that it is not so difficult to create complex drawings.

> New file, switch the units to meters and then set 30 meters long and 10 meters high. Display the whole page and set the grid to 0.2m each and activate "Snap on grid".

> Almost all (locomotive, windows, wagons …) are simply drawn from rectangles, which were filled in color:

⇨ Locomotives with **color gradient** type linear "black-white-black" horizontally, thus rotated by 90 °, chimneys with the same color gradient vertically, see page 68).

12. CH.: FOUNTAIN FILL — CORELDRAW 2020

Set with double-click a new color point and select light gray. Light gray you can easiest pick up, if you choose in the color menu the palettes.

Select the start and end colors as black.

50% = so is the color point exact in the middle.

- Use the **polygon tool** for the tip, the stars and the first chimney, each adjusting the number of corners.
- We already created a wheel in a separate drawing; the exercise can be found on page 54. **Copy the wheel** in this drawing and duplicate it horizontally by pressing the [Shift] button.
- For the **background,** draw two large rectangles, fill the upper with blue color, and fill the lower green and place backwards (property bar).
- Draw the smoke **clouds** with the freehand line. For this, switch off the grid and release the mouse only if you have reached again the starting point so that the figure is closed and can be filled.

Chapter 13

13. Special Fillings

To illustrate, some examples, which is presented below:

Full Color	Bitmaps (Photos)	Two Color	Vector

> In the case of the **Student Edition**, the number of prefabricated filling patterns is unfortunately greatly reduced. Some fill patterns are incorrectly sorted, e.g. "Apples" in full colors instead of bitmaps, so look at all fillings from time to time.

13.1 Full Color Fillings

Here you'll find a collection of various fillings.

Here you find graphic work from designers, e.g. color stripes or filled circles.

Assign a full-color filling:

Mark the object to fill and then the interactive fill tool-vector or bitmap fill:

Choose a category on left side and then click a pattern on the scroll list.

LINDEMANN B/H/IT © DIPL.-ING. (FH) PETER SCHIESSL   75

13.2 BITMAP-PATTERN FILLINGS

Here you will find fillings from real photos, e.g. from above photographed metal sheet or evergreen, too bad, with earlier versions there was a lot more choice, e.g. Coffee beans, cherries photographed from above, etc.

- With **Bitmap Pattern Fills,** experts from real photos can be used.
  - Bitmap, the file extension **bmp**, was used in early PC times by Windows for the Windows wallpaper images.
  - Thus, it is clear that we have to do it here with a **pixel-filling** so composed of points - with all the drawbacks, such as jagged edges.

Assign bitmap filling:

- Select another rectangle and apply a bitmap fill. As with the full-color pattern fill, just choose a fill from the preview window.
  - Note that you can then adjust the fill size and rotation on the lever handles.

Some are clippings of real photos and some are graphic work from designers, or both combined.

13.3 TWO-COLOR FILLING

- The fill pattern "**Two-colors**" is a painted pattern of only two colors in contrast to the colorful full-color fills.
  - The preference for **two color** is black and white, but you can choose other colors with the **color buttons**.

You can set the size of the tiles with the mouse at these handles.

Looks different? Use Window-Workspace-Default

13.4 TEXTURE FILL – THE CORELDRAW FILLINGS

These fillings drawn by graphic artists are the speciality of CorelDraw. Many of the Corel designed colored vector pattern fillings are very nice e.g. for a book title page.

- Mark a new rectangle, switch to the **Texture Fillings,** now you can choose a filling type in the **Property bar:**

Choose a collection here.

And then a filling type here.

More setting options in the filling menu:

Depending on the pattern there are other settings listed. Particularly interesting are the light, shadow, and brightness settings.

Choose a filling: Click here in the list once with the mouse, then scroll through the patterns.

In the other lists, you find many more fillings.

Changed fill patterns can be **stored** with the "+" in the pattern library or deleted with the "-".

Accidentally changed settings create new variations of the current pattern.

- **Texture # and # of bubbles**: click and try different variations of actual patterns, with more or fewer bubbles you have many possibilities for new filling patterns.
- Interesting also is the button **"Randomize"**, to generate new patterns.

13.5 POSTSCRIPT PATTERNS

Postscript is a standardized printer language developed in early 1980s from Adobe. The feature is that the print result is same between home office printer and print shop if both use postscript. Today most PDF formats, from Adobe, too, use it for same result.

➢ Choose the postscript patterns. You'll find some fillings consume less computing power. Look at the fill pattern; some are also colored.

13.6 The tile size

The pattern image is usually smaller than the object used to populate it. Therefore, the filling is made up of multiple images (**tiles**).

Tile

- With the bitmap and vector filling you can specify size with the mouse at the handles or in the menu by **Transformations**, but not with the Postscript fillings.
  - ↳ If the lock is closed, both dimensions are changed at the same time.
- The option "**Transform with object**" causes the filling to be scaled in case of subsequent size changes.

13.7 Make a New Pattern Fill

Bitmap fillings are from real **photos**. So you can set each photo or an area from a photo or graphic as a new pattern fill, e.g. photos from the internet. In the filling menu by **bitmap pattern fill** you find these symbols:

Load a photo from your storage media as a pattern fill.

- If you only want to save a **section of a photo** as a fill pattern: open in Photo-Paint, save under a different name, and crop to the desired section.
  - ↳ With **Object/Create/Pattern Fill** you can mark an area of your actual drawing and can set it as a new pattern fill.

13.8 Copy a Filling

If you want to re-record the filling of an object to assign it to another object, that comes with the pipette. The application is done simply, bearing in mind the selection menu:

- With the **Color Eyedropper** you can pick up a color, but not a filling, and insert it into another object.
- A filling pattern can be picked up with the **Attributes Eyedropper**; hold the mouse button on the Color Eyedropper symbol and hold down as the selection menu opens.
- Alternatively you can use the command "Edit/Copy Properties From…" e.g. to copy the filling from one object to another:
  - ↳ Mark the target first, then choose the above command and click on the object with the filling to copy.

14. ClipArt and Shadow

14.1 Insert ClipArt or Photos

To insert clipart or photo's you have following options:

- Photos already stored on your storage media can be inserted with **Import** into your actual drawing, or
- with more overview per drag & drop from the **Windows Explorer,** or
- you can use **Corel Connect**: here you can insert a photo from your storage media or insert content from Corel cloud.

Exercise Photo or ClipArt from the internet:

➢ Start your usual **Internet browser,** enter a search term at the top, e.g. **animal** or **plane**, confirm with Return and switch to the tab Photos or Pictures.

➢ Click on the desired photo first, so that the photo is displayed instead of the preview image, then **right-click** with **Save Image As**, and save it to your hard drive. You can now import it into CorelDRAW or Photo-Paint.

Exercise Photo or ClipArt with Corel Connect:

Since **Corel Connect**, which is part of Corel Suite, is currently very complicated to use, so short instructions necessary.

➢ **Window/Dockers/Connect-Browser,** enter a search term there in the search magnifier, e.g. plane, animal etc.

  ↳ If "**No content found**" appears, click the small arrow in front of it to return to the folder view and activate more folders.

  ↳ If photos are found and displayed, you can use this little triangle to go back to the folder display.

➢ Insert into the drawing: **drag** into the drawing area with the left mouse button pressed. If you have the photo, for example Drag on a rectangle to insert the photo as a fill for this rectangle. The **insert-in symbol** at the bottom of Connect is therefore actually unnecessary.

In addition, almost only a little content can be found on the **Home & Student Edition** online.

> Note the **copyright** of the owner – very important by publishing.

Notes on Corel Connect:

- On the top left you'll find **Flickr** (selection changes sometimes). These are online photo libraries. There you can search and download photos or post your own, some sites request a registration before using.
  - **Usage** in Connect: Put the checkmark next to Flickr in the folder view, then you will also find pictures for your search term.
- You can change the window's size at the left side of Connect and you can change the **photo-size** with the zoom-slider below in the Connect-window.

14.2 THE COREL-OBJECTS

Many objects (cropped people, animals or objects) that can be inserted into new drawings which are available on the Corel website. You should, therefore, take a look at them, as you can save a lot of work if you can use a finished object instead of cutting one out of a photo by yourself.

- You can find them in the Connect at **Window/Dockers/Connect Content**, then in this window type a **search term** at top, e.g. Oldtimers, plane, shark…
  - Next step: "**Get More**", click on the **download arrow**.
  - A window appears in which several **clip art and photo packages** can be downloaded, many of them free of charge,
  - unfortunately, many of them only for a fee, because as a Corel Oldi you wistfully think back to the times when, depending on the version, around 20,000 to 30,000 clip art were added to the Corel program package free of charge.
- For practice, you should **download and install** two or three free clip art collections. If you delete the initial search word Oldtimers, you will now find content in Connect, e.g. see picture right:

- Each of these objects can be **inserted** directly into a drawing without the background of the object becoming visible.
  - To insert, simply drag from the Connect onto the current image.

14.3 Exercise: Birthday Invitation

A exercise about inserting a clipart. With the countless finished clipart choices, it is necessary to draw only in the professional field.

> New drawing with DIN A4 landscape. Search in your web browser for example "**birthday cliparts**", then click on the Photos tab, click on appropriate clip art to enlarge and right-click/copy and paste in Corel.

14.3.1 Background for whole Page

> You can set a colored **background** easily by drawing a rectangle the same size as the page, filling it and placing it back. A prefabricated color fill was selected here (arrow in the preview image).

- If you draw the **background** first, you often accidentally get the background if you want to move an element.
    - This can be prevented as follows: Right mouse button on the background rectangle, then **Lock**. Unlock with same way with **right mouse button** on the object, then **Unlock**.

- With the command **Layout/Page Background** you can specify a single color as the background or load a photo by "Bitmap". But a color gradient filling is not possible there.
    - The "**Print and Export Background**" option is sometimes practical. If you disable this, you can use a background color to simulate a colored paper on the screen without printing this color.

14.3.2 Shadow Tool

Now the text follows. As we apply our first effect by assigning a shadow to it, the effect of this effort can be better seen against the background.

> Write the text as **two text blocks**, then arrange and set them separately as shown.

> Assign a matching **color gradient** to the text.

In the case of text, a deposited shadow is beautiful. Even a continuous shadow can be realized.

Open the selection menu for the effects and select the **Shadow**.

> From the text beginning with the mouse button pressed, draw an arrow which shows the provisional shadow or, at the top of the **property bar**, a presetting, e.g. "Medium Glow".

Shadow with the mouse at a sample text:

Change the **direction** and extent of the shadow.

Change the **transparency** of the shadow with this slider.

The Property bar for the drop shadow:

The "…glow" shadows are a very nice preset.

The opacity of the shadow is different depending on the color.

Flat Top Left
Perspective Top Right
Perspective Bottom Right
Perspective Bottom Left
Perspective Top Left
Small Glow
Medium Glow
Large Glow

The **shadow color** can be selected here. On a dark background, a lighter color makes sense.

In order for the shadow to be recognizable, the type "**outside**" is often selected, which means that the shadow runs outwards.

14.4 Insert ClipArt

A small advertisement as an exercise:

> ➢ New drawing with **half letter** size.
>
> ➢ Import a matching ClipArt, e.g. search in the web "**wine glass drawing**", adjust the size and move to the right position.

Set the **Grid** and use **guidelines** as edge markings. This helps to set the text to correct positions.

★ Draw an **ellipse** similar to the red dotted, then put it **behind** the clip art. (property bar).
★ Assign a **white filling** to the ellipse and set it slightly transparent, approx. 20%. Thus, the background is hidden something.

A **shadow** is nice for text most of the time. We have also added a shadow to the headline. Make sure the two shadows look much the same.

If the champagne glass has a background to be removed:

> ➢ If you use a clip art: Ungroup, then delete unwanted items, then group them again.
>
> ➢ For photos: Draw an ellipse over it as desired, select effect lens, lighten by e.g. 5% and "Fixed", then you can move this image section, delete the original image, we have created a section in ellipse size.
>
> ➢ Finally fill the text, arrange it and fill it in with color.
>
> ➢ As the background, draw a rectangle as large as the page and fill it. Here a radial color sequence was assigned.

Chapter 15

15. Interactive Menus

Interactive means that you can change settings directly with the mouse on the object instead of in a menu e.g. the direction of a color flow fill.

With the mouse, however, only the most important values can be set, also in the property bar, all other settings can be found in the respective menus.

15.1 Interactive Fill Pattern

In the case of the interactive filling, all the previously described can be set in the property bar. Fillings can thus be easily assigned. Here are some options.

➢ Draw a new rectangle in a new drawing and select the **Interactive Fill tool**.

➢ **Hold the mouse button** while drawing and you set the start and end points and the direction of the color gradient filling.

➢ At last, you can define the start and end **color**: Click on the boxes at the beginning and the end of the arrow and select one color at a time.

Now, these symbols appear in the property bar:

Select the **fill type** here, currently a linear color fill. You will also find the bitmaps and fill patterns here.

Preset fill patterns.

Select the **start and end color** for this on the respective color point.

A slider for the **transparency.**

Copy a filling: First select the target object, then this symbol, then click on the element whose filling is to be copied.

Looks different? Use Window-Workspace-Default

You can set the fill in the property bar or with the mouse on the object. Depending on the selected fill, other symbols are available that you already know from the previous chapters.

LINDEMANN B/H/IT © DIPL.-ING. (FH) PETER SCHIESSL   85

Adjust with the mouse:

You can also use the mouse to determine the starting and ending colors by clicking on a box of the **color gradient arrow** and clicking a color from the color palette.

Stretch the first color. Try: move to the other line = two colors.

Use the end handles to rotate, lengthen, or shorten the color gradient. If clicked, the color can also be adjusted.

Use the slider to determine the centre of the color transition.

Additional color points can be set by double-clicking.

15.2 INTERACTIVE MESH FILL

In this fill method, a mesh grid is placed in the selected object. Then a color can be drawn into each area. A color carpet is created.

➤ Select or draw a **new rectangle,** then hold down the left mouse button on the interactive fill symbol until the selection menu appears and change it to the mesh fill.

A mesh appears:

In each area of the grid, you can click or drag a **color** from the color palette using the left mouse button.

The stitches can even be **bent and moved** with the mouse.

You can also click on one of the **grid points** and then select a color. Thus, the area around the grid point is filled, which also results in pleasing fill effects

With **double-click** on a line you can set a new mesh line.

At the grid points you can reshape the object.

The following setting options appear in the Property Bar:

Here you can set more or fewer **grid lines**.

Choose the **color** of the selected mesh.

15.3 Interactive Transparency

In the Toolbox on left side you'll find the symbol for the transparency, so that the underlying objects glimmer through.

- Draw a new **rectangle**, fill with a color.
- Then draw an **ellipse** within this rectangle and assign it a fill color, too.
- Then choose the **Transparency tool** and either use the **mouse** to drag a transparency arrow within the ellipse or set the transparency in the **Property bar**.

In the case of transparency, fillings can also be selected as a mask:

No Transparency.

A **transparency slider** controls the transparency.

As with the fillings, **patterns** can be selected, but these are now translucent (see the following example with the wall filling).

Similar to color patterns, uniform, fountain, vector, **bitmap, bi-color** transparency can be selected, but now it is not a color fill, but a transparency.

Right side of property bar:

Edit Transparency.

With "**freeze**" the object can be moved, the background is retained.

Transparency with the mouse:

The slider for 50% transparency, adjust at the handles the size and angle.

Transparency with the two-color pattern "Wall":

The pattern size and direction can be set on the handles of the arrows.

15.4 Inserting Photos

This **interactive transparency** is particularly excellent when the effects are used to make a photo more and more dynamic.

This is what we try to do with a new exercise. On page 79, you have already inserted clipart. Likewise, you can insert photos same way.

> ➢ **New exercise**, looking for two photos on the web: Search for shark / flower meadow, click on each and let it display in normal size, right mouse button on / copy, paste in the corel, about the same size as the sheet of paper set, possibly margins of one photo cut something.

> ➢ Then use the **transparency tool** to drag a temporary transparency arrow:

Specify the transparency by an arrow.

You can then move the transparency arrow as you like, or change its length at the ends, making the transition wider or sharper.

The slider in the centre applies to the centre of transparency (50% transmittance).

> ➢ Then try the other transparency settings in the property bar such as Regular or Radial or Pattern, instead of linear transparency. Here, the flower image has been given a two-color transparency:

Try to **invert** the two-color-transparency.

Fourth Part

Shape

curve editing, text options and paragraph text

Something looks different? Use Window-Workspace-Default

16. Curve Editing

Now to the best of CorelDRAW: Self drawing!

- ♦ The moon, speakers, stars and figures in the following exercise we draw manual, and since this does not work out perfectly right away, we use the **Shape Tool** to reshape.

  ✋ With this tool, we can change the endpoints of lines or the points at which a curve changes direction.

For the Christmas tree exercise on page 70, you have already applied the Form tool, but now we explore its full capabilities.

16.1 Exercise: Party

This exercise is ideal for practicing copying with the mouse, including grouping, multiple fillings, and especially curves.

> For the stars, the moon and the figures, the curve processing is necessary, an excellent function with which even difficult curves can be adapted bit by bit.

> The background is a color gradient fill. To fill a page, a normal rectangle is drawn across the entire page. Then the rectangle obscures all other objects and has to be set backwards. So that we do not inadvertently move this while drawing, either fix it or draw it last.

Preparations:

- ➢ New file, DIN A5 or letter landscape, grid every 5 mm.
- ➢ A horizontal **guide line** for the floor so that all objects can be arranged at the same height.

The speaker:

- ➢ Draw a rectangle as a speaker cabinet:
  - ★ Make it wide enough that in the middle is a grid row, so that the individual loudspeaker chassis can be drawn easily in the middle.
- ➢ Draw a **chassis** as a circle with a thick, different colored line:
  - ✎ Start in the middle of the chassis with the first point, hold [Ctrl] and [Shift] = Circle around the first point.
- ➢ Assign a **radial color gradient** fill, then copy the first circle in the middle and reduce it:
  - ✎ Hold the circle at a corner touch point, resize it while holding down [Shift] and click the **right mouse button** for copying.
  - ★ Switch off the line for this small inner circle.
- ➢ **Group on chassis**, then you can copy it easily and modify the size matching your imaginations.
- ➢ When a loudspeaker is ready, assign the fill to the enclosure and group it completely. Do not redo the second speaker - just copy it.

16.2 The Stars – Move the Turn Points

1. Draw a **star**: Deactivate grid, click start and end point once, otherwise double-click.
2. Now use the **Shape Tool** to move the corner points until the star looks halfway like a star (this can also be done with the Pick Tool).

- ➢ Fill the star, then copy the star several times, and rotate or resize each copy to vary their appearance.

This is a good exercise. But later you can use more easy stars from symbol fonts (see p. 60), or draw it with the **Polygon Tool,** or use the polyline (then only double-click first and last point, otherwise single click).

16.3 The Moon - Circle Segments

To draw the moon, we cut circular segments out of two circles and then connect them to one element to fill the moon.

- ➢ Draw **one circle** (with pressed [Ctrl]-button) and copy it slightly offset:

Now these red marked circle parts have to be cut off.

➢ When the **Shape Tool** is selected, click a circle. At the top of the circle, a small dot appears (not the eight handle points on the outside!).

Open the circle at this small point a little and look at the line that remains. Just try and then move the line accordingly

[Alt]-Y

Now temporarily disable "**Align to Grid**" to allow the circular segments to meet.

At this end, drag the circle to the intersection point.

Almost done.
Now drag the other end to the intersection of the two circles.

Cake piece or bow:

Somewhere outside the circle let go, and Corel draws no lines to the center - a **circular arc arises**.

What are these lines?
A cake piece?

Somewhere within the circle let the mouse go, and the lines to the center of the circle are there - a **cake piece**.

No unnecessary thoughts needed to see **which part is preserved**. Open something, then see in which direction it goes.

➢ Now transform the second circle to the arc and the moon is finished.

Well, that was once a very useful drawing function.

16.4 Combine to Fill

Filling is usually not yet possible, because for Corel there are only two circular arcs, which have nothing to do with each other. So we must tell Corel that this is a connected figure, a moon:

- ➢ Mark both arcs and **combine** them.
  - ✥ This can be done with a symbol in the property bar, as soon as several objects are selected, in the menu with **Object/Combine** or with Shortcut **[Ctrl]-L**.

[Ctrl]-L

For marking:

- ♦ If you press [Shift], you can select several objects by clicking on them.
  - ✥ As long as you press the [Shift] key, you can also delete a marking.
  - ✥ Note the message in the status bar at the bottom of the Corel window:
    "2 Objects Selected on Layer 1".

The difference between Group and Combine:

- ♦ **Group** summarizes objects to an element.
- ♦ **Combine** if you want to fill between two objects.

16.5 Closing of the Figure

In most situations, it is still not enough to fill the moon.

- ➢ Try it by clicking on a color of the color palette with the right mouse button.

Filling is not yet possible because the endpoints of the two arcs are not yet exactly met. Zoom in on the endpoints and you will see it in your drawing.

There we have the evil. But this can be corrected with the **Shape Tool**.

You can only use the Form tool if the arcs have previously been marked with the **Pick Tool** or are already combined.

Use the **Shape Tool** to draw a marker frame so large that both endpoints of the arcs are completely included.

Now the necessary commands appear in the Property Bar:

If the endpoints of both curves are not touching, this easy-to-recognize symbol "**Join two nodes**" (nodes = turnpoints) is highlighted.

The opposite, "**Break Curve**" is active when closed nodes are selected.

Is it time to fill the moon? If not, only these two sources of error can be considered:

- The arcs are **not yet combined** or inadvertently grouped instead.
- The **endpoints are not closed**. Check with a strong zoom, and if necessary, repeat the procedure as described above.

16.6 ADD TURNPOINTS FOR THE NOSE

The moon looks quite nice, but can be even more beautiful. We'll add a big nose.

Features of the Shape Tool:

All possible objects can be added or changed at any time. Even very difficult bodies can be drawn piece by piece.

➢ A turning point is already quite present in the middle. Click on this point and choose **Cusp Node** in the property bar, so that we get sharp corners and no round curves.

➢ We will **add a point** a little more here with the Shape Tool.
  - The fastest method is to add a new point by double-clicking on the curve line. This also immediately switch to a Cusp Node point.
  - Other method: use the **Shape Tool** to set a provisional point, then press the + in the property bar or on the keyboard for a new point. Only then is the turning point actually set.

- ➤ Now you can use the mouse to draw the curve between the two new turning points and pull it out.
    - ✎ Do not touch the two levers, since it is then double work, but pull out the curve in the middle between the two turning points.

First bulge in the **middle**, then adjust the nose more appropriately at these arrows (levers, tangents). Each turning point has two arrows for the two directions.

Lever for fine adjustment.

A nose is formed. More about the levers in the next chapter. Under the nose, you could just as well add a mouth.

16.7 THE FIGURES – ADAPT THEIR SHAPE

Also, line figures can not be filled as long as there is not a closed line around.

Proceed as follows:

- ➤ Draw approximately the bodies.
    - ✎ With polylines or normal line and double-click.
- ➤ As with the stars, use the **Shape Tool** to make the figures close enough to correct.
- ➤ Try, if you can, to **fill** the figures.
    - ✎ If not, as by the moon, close the turning points with the Shape Tool until filling is possible.
- ➤ Only when the bodies are already filled, then we will supplement the **arms:**

Set with the **Shape Tool** a new point with double-click, then click on the line and **convert to curve**, then pull out.

Set other points, switch to cusp node and pull out.

Also set a point and pull out.

➢ **Hands and heads** (ellipses) at high zoom:

Draw with **Freehand Tool**, then push and put backwards.

Draw with **Freehand Tool**, then push to head and put in front.

➢ We also draw the feet very simply with the **Freehand Tool**:

➢ With **high zoom** you can draw the eyes, mouth and nose with the tools you know (ellipses, freehand, curve lines) if you want.

 ✎ How eyes, noses and mouths can be drawn better follows in the next chapter step by step. Those who want can return to this drawing later to replace the eyes, mouth and nose with the later lessons.

➢ At the end, **group** each figure to make it an element, and the arrangement cannot be accidentally destroyed.

As an alternative, you could use characters from a symbolic font, or search for suitable clipart from the Corel clipart database or from the Internet.

Also, symbols and clipart can be changed with the **shape tool**. Sometimes necessary to ungroup them before redrawing is possible.

Notes: ....
....
....
....
....
....
....
....
....

17. THE SNAKE – CURVES TOTAL

Compared to the snake, all the previous practice was only a small pre-exercise. But no fear, it will not be much more difficult; however, you will now realize how powerful the **Shape Tool** is.

➢ New drawing, size first 100 mm wide, 210 mm height.
  ★ Set the **Grid** every 5 mm and activate align on grid and set guidelines as border lines by 10, 90 vertically and 10, 150 horizontally.

Looks different? Use Window/ Workspace/Default

In addition to the curve processing for the snake, we will try the following functions for text:
- Insert **special characters** in text,
- Text with **shadow**,
- **Align** text to object.

Adventure ▶ Fun ▶ Sports Ltd.
321 Pearl Street
New York, New York, 10038 USA
Phone +1-123-123-4566
Fax: +1-123-123-4566-50

17.1 First Preliminary Exercise

So that it is not too difficult, we begin with only one curve.

- ➤ Draw a straight line in the side edge, approx. 5 cm long.
- ➤ Click with the **Shape Tool** in the middle of the line.
- ➤ Because we have selected a line, the **Convert to Curve button** is active. Click it to make a curve out of the line:

Switch to curve, left switch to line.

For turning points: cusp, smooth, symmetric.

Do not hold the line by the levers, but rather in the middle and bend them to a **curve**.

The levers appear when you click an end point.

More to try:

- ➤ Turn one of the **levers** until the curve becomes an "S":

- ➤ **Move** an initial point of the curve.

- ➤ Turn one of the levers and observe the effect.

- ➤ Pull a lever all the way out - the curve bulges - and then very small - the curve is easy to bounce.

Levers are tangents! About the levers:

Levers

- ♦ **Long levers** complicate the handling in practice.
- ♦ In addition, you can see that two curves (S) can be made from one stretch.
- ♦ We therefore need only very few turning points.
- ♦ Too many turning points make the work much more difficult!

17.2 Second Preliminary Exercise

Now you know the levers a little bit. In the next exercise we go one step further.

Preparation:

> ➢ Delete the first curve that has just been drawn.
> ➢ Draw **two lines**, double-click at the intersection:

> ➢ Convert both lines to **curves**.
>> ✎ You can use the shape tool to draw a selection frame to select both lines at once and convert them to curves.

Curves without edges:

Now the point of intersection of the two curves is important, because there, finally, no edge should remain. This is achieved by aligning the levers to a line as shown in the following figure.

> ➢ **Bend** the curves as shown to make the levers appear. First touch the curves in the middle and bend them out:

If you are straightening these levers straight, the curve has no kink, since the levers are tangents. This is automatically done with "**Smooth Node**".

Please note again:
A line produces two curves.
Do not draw too many lines on the snake! This results in too many nodes and that means chaos!

To exercise the levers, we have just **smoothed** a curve by hand. Corel does the same smoothing with the functions mentioned. If these are switched on, you cannot pull an acute angle like the nose.

Smooth knots, ideal for the snake, since no "kink" is possible. The right is also symmetrical.

Cusp nodes e.g. for the tip of a fish fin.

The **current setting** cannot be selected, so it is only displayed weakly.

Symmetrical as smoothed, but the two levers are automatically the same length. Try to extend a lever.

17.3 Serious Case: The Snake

The snake is not a problem if you remember not to draw too many lines. Other points could be supplemented at any time by the + or with a double-click, but too many turning points lead to a chaos of levers.

You will see that the following figure with the red line easily turns into the green snake with round curves.

- ➢ Delete the previous curves.
- ➢ Draw the red lines by double-clicking on one piece.

The **grid** should be switched off for such freehand drawings.

Either with **lines** =
continue with double-click, stop with single click
or with the **Polyline** = continue with single click and stop with double-click.

- ➢ If necessary, move the turning points appropriately.

Convert lines to curves:

- ➢ You can **convert** several lines at once to curves by marking them with a large selection frame with the **Shape Tool**, then **switch to curves**.

Select the turning points, and assign the desired type:

- ➢ On the head we need pointed points (cusp node), so mark the head with a selection frame and switch to **cusp node** (they are probably already pointed), and the same for the end point.
- ➢ Then mark the **fuselage** (without head and end) and select "**smoothed**" in the property bar. The turning points are automatically smoothed, and the desired round contours are created.

The function "**smoothed**" helps for nice round curves, only at the tip of the tail and at the head are some pointed points necessary.

- ➢ **Modify** the curves further until the snake shape fits.
  - ✎ The easiest way to do this is to touch the corners in the middle, not the levers.
- ➢ **Save** as "Snake" – we need this later again for making a flyer.

If it does not go as expected, there are probably still **open points**. Then close these points as described in Chapter 16.5.

What you might need:

- ♦ **Add Points**: with double-click (or "+").
- ♦ **Delete Points**: Mark the point and click "–" in the Property Bar or on the keyboard.
- ♦ **Move Points**: with the **Shape Tool** every time possible.

17.4 THE HEAD AND THE POINTS

The head shape is designed just like the snake body:
- By strong zoom convert the lines to curves and buckle out.

The eyes consist of two ellipses:

The easiest way is to draw them first in the empty area next to the head, increasing this area as much as possible.

- Increase line thickness at the outer edge, both fill color. Adjust **colors** for both.
- Finish, then **group** to one eye, rotate and fit in the right place.
- Do not redo the **second eye**, but copy the first (with the right mouse button), then move and then rotate.

The hair is the easiest:
- Draw three **lines**, convert them to curves and bend them appropriately.
- Line thickness, color, and round end pieces in the line menu.
- **Group** the three hairs to an object.

The mouth:
- Draw **two lines** one at a time: Click, move mouse away and double-click, and return to the starting point,
- **convert** to curves and bend them appropriately.
- Increase the line **thickness**, select Fill and line color.
- If the filling does not work, close the points.

On the left and right, set two points, switch to sharp to make the center part more bulging.

- Finally, supplement the tongue and group all elements.
- Now the mouth can be rotated and positioned correctly.

Do not draw on other objects, but

in a vacancy or in a separate drawing. Only when an object is ready, group it and move it to the correct position. Adjust the size and rotation.

We continue in the next chapter with **text and pictures**.

18. TEXT EDITING

Whether it is a poster, a cover page or a promotional brochure, text almost always occurs.

Corel offers two types of text editing:

- The **Graphic text** with the text tool (which you have done so far) for short texts that can be placed and rotated as desired.
- The **Paragraph text** to write longer texts as in a text program. Even styles can be assigned.

In the following exercise, we will supplement the text to the snake and will also **fit the text to the snake** as shown in the picture and in other various ways.

18.1 PRODUCING SHADOWS

- Write with the Text Tool: AFS.
- Use the mouse or the property bar to enlarge it, but do not rotate.

A simple **monochrome shadow** is very nice and is used more often in professional work than special effects.

For this we will **copy the text** and move it slightly. Then the color is changed for text and shadow and the shadow is finished.

- For copying and accurate moving, the menu **Window/Dockers/Transform** with Position is ideal.

18. Ch.: Text Editing — CorelDRAW 2020

With Window/Dockers/Transform exact values can be specified:

[Alt]-F7

Transform — Position, Rotate, Scale and Mirror, Resize, Tilt.

Position
- X: 0,1"
- Y: 0,15"
- ✔ Relative Position
- Copies: 0
- Apply

Set horizontal and vertical offset, then specify 1 copy and "**Apply**". This gives you a slightly offset copy.

Press "**Apply**" to "**0 copies**" to move the copy step by step.
If you set the **minus** sign in front of the values, the elements can also be **pushed back**.

Move an offset **copy (1)** or move the object (**0 copies**) or **multiple copies**, which are moved by the specified posi-

- ➢ Move the new object to the back (**Object/Order/Back one**) and change the color.
- ➢ The shadow is finished, finally the two different colored texts can be **grouped** into one element.
- ➢ Write "**Adventure Fun Sports**" with two empty keys between the words because a special character will be placed there.

We want to turn AFS and Adventure … at the same angle:

By means of the **Property Bar**, we can rotate different objects at the same angle.

- ➢ You can rotate first with the mouse approximately the way you want, and then change it to the next even value in the Property Bar, e.g. to 50 ° instead of 50.317.

X: 104,406 mm | 38,813 mm | 100,0 %
Y: 96,922 mm | 6,155 mm | 100,0 %
↻ 0,0 | Arial | 24 pt

Enter or correct the **rotation angle**. A rotation can also be reset to 0°.

Even with the text selected, the rotation angle is displayed next to the text settings in the property bar.

- ➢ Without the Property Bar, the option remains over this handy menu **Window/Dockers/Transform** by Rotate.
  - ↳ Here, for example, set a rotation of 10 °, then press "**Assign**" several times until the angle of rotation fits.
  - ↳ The angle of rotation is thus known and can be assigned exactly the same to other objects.

18.2 INSERT SPECIAL CHARACTERS

Now we insert symbol fonts between: Adventure Fun Sports

- ➢ Choose the **Text Tool** and set the cursor between two words (we have prepared with two space bars between the words).
- ➢ With **Text/Glyphen** or **[Ctrl]-[F11]** you can open the special character window
- ➢ there you can select a special font, e.g. **Wingdings**. You can drag a symbol on the text or insert with double-click.
  - ★ Move the cursor to the next position with the directional buttons and double-click on the symbol again.

Adventure ⮕ Fun⮕ Sports

18.3 COLOR VARIETY

In this text, the **initial letters** are to be displayed in a different color:

- ➢ Select **Text Tool**, click on text and mark the first letter of adventure, then use the mouse to assign a different color from the color palette.

Marking a letter, you have these possibilities:

- ♦ With the mouse, it requires fingertip feeling to mark exactly one letter.
- ♦ Holding down the **[Shift]** key and a directional key will make it easier.
  - ✎ And you can also unmark if you have marked too much as long as you hold down the [Shift] key with the directional key in other direction.

The color is only changed for the selected text.

18.4 ALIGN TEXT TO AN OBJECT

With this function **"Fit Text to Path"**, text can be written to an object, e.g. at our snake. Let's try it:

- ➢ The **grouping** of the snake must be cancelled beforehand.
- ➢ Click on the text "Adventure ..." and select **Text/Fit Text to Path**.
- ➢ The mouse arrow changes to a bigger arrow, when you move the mouse near the snake, a **preview** is displayed.
  - ✎ Move the mouse near the queue until arranged as desired, then confirm with a mouse click.
  - ✎ The **initial position** and the **distance** from the route can be subsequently adjusted in the Property Bar.

You can **change the arrangement** at any time in the Property Bar if text and object are selected:

How to arrange? Straight letters or as set here also correspondingly rotated.

Distance text to object.

Move text along the route for optimal placement.

Tick Snapping:

- For example, if set at 5mm, the target position can still be freely selected with the mouse, but at a distance of 5mm, this locks a little, even afterwards during the movement.

If the text is placed on the wrong side, mirror it:
Text can also be arranged below.

18.5 Add The Address

Fill in the address at the bottom of the picture.

> Write the **Headline** separate and fit left and right side to the Guidelines.
> Then make two blocks of **Paragraph Text**, align one to the left Guideline and text left aligned, the other to the right Guideline and the text inside right-aligned.
>> The feature with Paragraph Text is so you can **align easy and exactly** to left and right Guideline. With Graphic Text this is not easy to adjust exactly because Corel counts coordinates for the center point of it.

Adventure ➲ Fun ➲ Sports Ltd.

125 Barclay Street
New York, NY 10007
United States

Phone: (212) 888-1111
Fax: (212) 888-1114
www.adv-fun-sports.com
Email: sample@adv-fun-sports.com

18.6 Other Adjustments for Text

The Property Bar is very handy, but only the most important settings are available. The Property Bar for text you'll find in Chapter 10.1.1.

- The complete menu with all settings for text can be found on these paths:
  - **right mouse button** on the text, then **Properties**
  - or open with **Window/Toolbar/Text** the toolbar for text
  - or **Text/Text**: in this menu you will also find the **position** or **fractional numbers**,
  - the shortcut **[Ctrl]-T** opens this menu, too,
  - or use the symbol in the Property Bar to see left border.

[Ctrl]-t

This extensive and unfortunately confusing setting menu for text will be presented on the next page.

The Docker Text/Text:

The three areas of **Characters**, **Paragraphs** and **Frames** can be flipped open and closed by clicking on them.

On the top font, font type and font size.

Kerning follows in the second book.

Above can be selected the fill for the text, center for the text background and the bottom line color.

Open the menu by clicking on "…"

Various font settings, e.g. superscript. Depending on the font not all available.

Various **Caps**.

This setting menu is very extensive and therefore unfortunately also somewhat unclear.

Now we still need paragraph formatting, this mostly applies to Paragraph text:

Orientation left, centred, right, block set, strong block set also for the last line.

Disable alignment.

Line spacing, in percent or point.

Feed: Left, for the first line and from the right, only for Paragraph Text.

Distance before / after the paragraph.

The above menu is also accessible via **Windows/Dockers/Text** or with **[Ctrl] -T**.

More about the text settings:

- The setting in **percentage of the character size** has the advantage that the setting is adapted automatically if you change the font size.
- Depending on the font selected, not all options are possible, e.g. some fonts cannot be set bold or italic.
- Text/Text Properties, [Ctrl]-[Shift]-T or in the Property Bar **ab|** opens a small text screen (text editor) in which you can correct, write and format the text - helpful if the text is distorted with effects.

18.7 OTHER TEXT HELPS

- Corel provides all the tools of a good word processing program that you will find in **Text/Writing Tools**:
  - a Spell Checker,
  - a Grammar Checker and
  - **Thesaurus,** a dictionary for synonyms. Here you can search for similar terms to a word.
  - the **QuickCorrect**, which opens a window in which this automatic correction can be adjusted,
  - the **language** can also be chosen here so that the spelling check also works for foreign-language texts.

About QuickCorrect:

The **QuickCorrect** is similar the **AutoCorrekt** in MS Word.

- With "**Capitalize first letter of sentences**" the first letter of a sentence is also capitalized after each abbreviation, since CorelDRAW starts a new sentence after each point. This option is disabled for Corel by default. If the capitalization is corrected once after an abbreviation, Corel accepts this.
- With "**Change straight quotes to typographic quotes**" Corel changes to "abc" instead of "abc".
- "**Replace text while typing**" automatically replaces the standard errors in the list below with the entered texts.
  - Other abbreviations, e.g. for a company name, can be supplemented. In the case of "**Replace**:", enter an abbreviation or an incorrect spelling, enter the detailed or correct spelling in "**With**:" and save it with "**Add**".
  - If you often have unwanted replacements, you should **disable** this feature. If you want to use this function, it is worthwhile to maintain the replacement list.

Note: ....
....
....
....

Chapter 19

19. THE PARAGRAPH TEXT

Paragraph text is the second type of text editing in CorelDRAW. While graphic text behaves as a drawing element, paragraph text is arranged in a text frame.

Paragraph text is, so to speak, a small text program, which we can open in a Corel graphic. This text is set within a frame for the delineation.

paragraph text for big amounts of text.

You start the Paragraph Text as follows:

- Press as usual the text symbol. Then:
  - Click in the drawing to write **Graphic Text** or
  - Draw a Paragraph Text frame like a rectangle with the mouse button pressed.
- **Caution, do not draw empty Paragraph Text frames!**
  - Draw a Paragraph frame only if this is the intention.
  - Otherwise, immediately switch back from the **Text Tool** to the **Pick Tool** arrow, otherwise you would use the text tool instead of the Pick Tool and create an empty text frame.

Empty quantity text frames are indicated by dashed lines. Delete any accidentally drawn frames: **Click on it with Pick Tool – [Del].**

Empty Paragraph Text frames: *Paragraph Text frames with text:*

19.1 CONVERTING TEXT

You can convert graphic text to paragraph text and vice versa. This is displayed in the Text Menu, in the scrolling menu with the right mouse button or with the keyboard truncation [Ctrl]-F8.

[Ctrl]-F8

Conditions:
- Mark the text with the **Pick Tool**, not with the Text Tool.
- With **Paragraph text,** the text frame does not have to be so big that the text is completely visible.

19.2 Exercise: Business Card

To get a better understanding of the Paragraph Text, we will create a small business card. This is how it will go:

> ➢ New drawing, size 80X60 mm or 30"x20", adjust the grid to 1 mm or 0.2" distance – for a small drawing we need a fine grid distance.

Because we are printing on colored paper, we choose a paper color:

> ➢ **Layout/Page Background**, then choose with "**Solid:**" the color palette **Pantone CMYK Coated** by Process.

Chose here a **Pantone-Palette:** Palette bibliotheca/Process/Pantone.

Make a pre-selection in the color bar, then click a color on the left.

For example, if you use the color number, e.g. in the side margin and forward it to the printing office, the color exactly matches.

> ➢ Switch off "**Print and Export Background**", so that the set paper color is not printed – if the print shop will use paper in this color.
>> ✎ It is a good practice to better assess ink composition on the screen when printing on colored paper.

The two lines above and below are simple rectangles with a color gradient fill:

> ➢ Place the **Guidelines** 4 mm or 1.5" apart from the side edge.
> ➢ Draw a **rectangle,** turn the outline off (with the right mouse button at the top of the color palette with the X) and
> ➢ fill with a **gradient color filling** similar to the one shown.

Now we will copy and flip the rectangle once, which gives the copy a precisely swapped color fill (Object/Transform/Scale and Mirror).

Here you can also change the **size**.

Flip both horizontally and vertically, then "**Apply**". The copy is exactly above the original, simply push away.

This is also possible by rotating the angle by 180° in the fill menu and assigning this fill to the copy.

Now the two rectangles with the color gradients are there.

1 for one copy.

➢ Use the text tool "A" to draw a border between the help lines and the rectangle and enter the text.

↳ Since this frame is docked to the left and right of the help lines, the centering of the text is easier than with the graphic text.

19.3 HANDLING WITH THE PARAGRAPH TEXT FRAMES

♦ Too much or too big of text or a **too small text frame** will cause the text to be displayed only partially or not.

↳ Always pull the frame down and right **much larger** than necessary until the text is set correctly. Only if the text is finished, then reduce the size of the text frame.

↳ An alternative is the command "**Text/Paragraph Text Frame/Fit Text to Frame**", also accessible by right-clicking on the frame, so the font size is automatically adjusted so that the text fills the frame.

You can move text frames like a normal rectangle or enlarge them at the **handles**.

Click the right side of this symbol and the text can be **locked or compressed**.

Click the left side of this symbol to change the line **spacing**.

Click and drag a new text frame, or click a different text frame (or rectangle), then the text continues in the other frame.

➢ **Format** the business card as shown. Always select the appropriate text.

19.4 PRINT FROM CORELDRAW

As in any program, you can print on these paths:
File/Print / with the Symbol / [Ctrl]-P.

- On the tab "**General**", the printer can be selected and the desired print quality can be set by "**Preferences…**".
  - With "**Page:**" you can choose **Landscape** or **Portrait**.

With the "**Home & Student**" Edition you have an easier print menu; there you can only choose with "**Imposition layout**" some preferences for label print. By the full edition you can set the quantity of rows and columns with "**Page Layout**".

On the tab "Layout" you can specify the arrangement to print.

Print original size or fit to paper size?

Tiled Pages: printed on several sheets, which are subsequently glued together.

Edit opens the settings menu with preview.

With the Preview the printout can be optimally prepared.

Choose „Edit" by Imposition Layout for the settings:

Switch to "Edit Gutters & Finishing" and you can set the distances in the preview.

Set column and line numbers.

With the "+" you can save your settings and then select it later here from the drop-down list.

Back to Print Menu.

> Close this menu, switch on the Preview and it if all matches, **print** it out.

Another method, with a bit of manual work, but more obvious, is to specify the columns and lines with **Guidelines**, and to copy the first completed business card into the other cells before printing, would also go automatically with the transform menu.

Chapter 20

20. PICTURES AND TEXT

You already know the word processing, including Paragraph text, the snake is already drawn and how pictures are inserted has already been explained in the exercise on page 79. Consequently, the prospectus should now be finished without any problems.

It is supposed to be a folded sheet with 5 folded columns. So that the exercise does not take too long, this is cut here on three sides. And the original images were replaced by images from the Web.

- ➢ **Open** the exercise **Snake** from Chapter 17 and save it under the name AFS folder.
- ➢ Instead of one page, we now need to set up three, that is, **page format** three times as wide as **300 mm**.
- ➢ You can now set the following **vertical Guidelines**: 10, 90/110, 190/210, 290. In the case of known coordinates, the Guideline menu is advantageous: Right mouse button on the **ruler**, then select "**Guidelines Setup…**".
- ➢ Mark the **snake side** (snake and address text) with a large marking frame (Pick Tool) and drag it to the right page.

Two more pages that are now filled. Guidelines indicate the margins: 10, 90; 110, 190; 210, 290 mm.

Draw a **line** over the edge and draw it a little too thick, because the brochure will later be cut off obliquely.

Auxiliary Guidelines mark the area for the text fields and photos, e.g. at 10, 70, 80, 135, 150.

At 100 and 200 the prospectus is folded. Draw a bright, dashed line as a folding aid at 100 and 200.

20.1 INSERT PHOTOS

Now we have three sides, two of which are still empty.

> ➢ Now we search for photos on the Internet: start an **Internet browser** and search e.g. by www.msn.com or www.google.com, matching photos for our flyer as "**travel**" or "**beach**" or "**scuba**" and switch to "**photos**".
>
> ➢ Open suitable photos, copy with **right mouse button-copy** and insert in Corel, also with right mouse button or the symbol.
>
> ✦ If you save the photos on your hard drive, you could insert it in CorelDRAW the following ways: using the symbol "**Import**", from Corel **Connect**, or open the folder in the **Windows Explorer** and drag into CorelDRAW.
>
> ➢ Adjust the size roughly and move it to the desired position with the left top handle matching to the Guidelines, then finish by moving the size to the right bottom Guideline corner.
>
> ✦ Change the **size of images** only at the corner points, otherwise the size ratio will be distorted. If this happens, immediately undo or re-import the image.

Arrangement of sample pictures:

Do not look for the original example photos, but similar ones from the Internet.

Bathing and Adventure Holiday

1 — Move first to this corner point of the Guidelines.

2 — Second to this corner point of the Guidelines.

20.2 CUT EDGE AREAS OF PHOTOS

Most times the size ratio doesn't exactly match our photo area. Simply enlarging or compressing is sometimes possible, but sometimes the size ratio gets disturbed visibly. Then we cut the edge areas with the **Shape** or **Crop Tool**:

Use the **Shape Tool** to drag the edge point to the help line corner to cut the image.

Also possible with the **Crop Tool** to mark the remaining area and confirm with return.

116 LINDEMANN B/H/IT © DIPL.-ING. (FH) PETER SCHIESSL

20.3 Insert Paragraph Text

➢ Drag a Guideline over the first image so that all the sets of text frames can be arranged at the same height, then set them.

a Paragraph Text frame over the column, write the heading, and center it.

Paragraph Text frames can be resized or moved like rectangles at the handles.

A set of Paragraph Text frames for the description text. Set this with 12 pt and block set.

Between paragraphs, a space is positively noticeable. How this is set, you will see below.

20.4 Text Formatting and Hyphenation

You can format the Paragraph Text similar to the Graphic Text, except that all setting options for a good writing program are available for the Paragraph Text. You will find most of the settings in the **Properties bar**.

For further paragraph settings, use the A symbol:

Line spacing

Paragraph indent: Left, first line indent and right.

Paragraph spacing before and after the paragraph.

Hyphenation

By **Text/Use Hyphenation** you can activate it, which is particularly recommended for Paragraph Text.

20.5 ADD A PAGE

The back of the page will be filled with text and images like the first page, where we insert a normal page and print it later in two stages: first the front, turn the paper, and then the backside unless the printer can duplex.

At the bottom left you can add (empty) pages:

This + is used to add a new page **before** the current page.

This + is used to add a new page **after** the current page.

The quantity of pages.

➢ Add another page. If done, you can change the pages at the bottom of the page:

To the last page.

Click to select a page.

➢ Copy the **top line** to the back and mirror it.
➢ Add more photos from the Internet and set in the desired positions, then add sample text as shown, matching your pictures, of course.

Find matching photos and arrange them in the columns:

The Dream of Flying

Get into the air!
Whether with the paraglider, parachute, or as a glider or parachute, a paragliding safari, with hot air balloon, bungeejumping or bodyflying.

Get out into Nature

Riding with the horse or with the engine sled in Canada, Germany, Austria, Italy, France, USA etc. Climbing, adventure camps, spelunking (caves) etc.

Set the font size, type etc. again and again manually? First copy a selected text frame, then overwrite the text, or copy the text settings with **Edit/Copy Properties From...**

As in a good writing program, we can store the text settings in one **style** and assign them to other paragraphs as often as you want. This is presented in our progress book filled with more professional exercises.

20.6 Edit Photos

In CorelDRAW, you can cut the edges of the image with the **Shape Tool**, while marking two handles with a selection frame so that it is not crooked.

With **Effects/Adjust** you'll find the commands to change the brightness, contrast and more and with **Bitmaps** you'll find all effects for photos from Corel Photo-Paint. In our book about **Corel PHOTO-PAINT** you will find a description of these numerous effects for photos. If you press the right mouse button on a picture and select **Edit bitmap**, PHOTO-PAINT is started.

Photo-Paint

The important icons of the Property bar for photos:

[Toolbar image with labels: Change Position, Change Size, Rotate, Open the photo in Photo-Paint to modify, Mirror, Vectorize = Transform in a drawing, For/back, Cut, Resample Bitmap, Color mask, Wrap text]

- **Rotate**: images can be rotated, which is also possible with the mouse as with any other element.
- **Photo-Paint** is the program for photos. All images (photos) in the computer are so-called pixel images. Therefore, editing is quite different from CorelDRAW, so a separate program is used. More about Corel PHOTO-PAINT in our book on this program.
- **Vectorize**: This allows pixel images to be converted into vector drawings, which means that photos can be converted into graphics, which usually does not yield any results that would be suitable for further processing since too many lines and turning points are created.

In the menu Bitmaps:

- **Resample**: a menu appears in which you can reduce the size or resolution (= number of pixels = dpi = dots per inch) of a photo, which naturally also decreases the quality (sharpness) in addition to the file size.
- **Bitmap Mask**: in the window that appears, you can use the Eyedropper Tool to pick up colors from the image to hide these colors.
  - ✎ This is convenient to hide e.g. a largely monochrome background.
  - ✎ The reverse way that the recorded colors remain visible is also possible.

Transparent

- **Right mouse click/Wrap Paragraph Text**: You can select whether the text is to run outside or over (= every click change) for graphic elements or photos. Over the photo e.g. to use an image as a background.

Fifth Part

Effects

for Text and Extrusion

---

21. Effects for Text

For a better overview, we begin with the effects, which are mainly suitable for text. Further effects follow in the progress band.

> **Copy** each sample text a few times so you have enough material to try out!

21.1 Interactive Effects

Most of the effects can be found as interactive menus on the left in the toolbox:

Press and hold down the left mouse button to open the selection menu: **shadow, contour, blend, distort, envelope, extrude.**

Shadow
Contour
Blend
Distort
Envelope
Extrude
Block Shadow

Transparency effects are not in this effects menu, you find them separate under this icon:

Block shadow: New since CorelDRAW 2019.

With this **+**, the displayed symbols and submenus can be selected, more precisely deselected, since all symbols are activated.

In these interactive menus, you can specify the settings in the property bar or by holding down the left mouse button.

The old method by means of a command for effects is however at the beginning at least more clearly, since a menu is opened, in which the setting possibilities are clearly recognizable.

Therefore, we start with the **Effects menu**, the interactive commands are described in the progress band, but can also be applied without guidance if the effects are known.

File   Edit   View   Layout   Object   **Effects**   Bitmaps   Text   Table   Tools   Window   Help

Examples of the interactive effects and their applications can be found in Chapter 15 on page 85.

21.2 Move Letters

The easiest effect: letters can be positioned anywhere with the left mouse button (only in graphic text).

> ➢ New graphic and write as Graphic Text: **Hello!** Copy it a couple times.
> ➢ Choose the **Shape Tool** and you can move letters at the handle points.

Use the Shape Tool to pull letters apart:

For multi-line text, you can change the **line spacing** here.

At this symbol, text can be stretched or compressed.

21.3 Add Perspective

> ➢ Choose another copy of the **sample text**.
> ➢ Start with: **Object/Add Perspective**.

Corel switches to the shape tool and you can move points with the mouse the corner so that a perspective can be set.

Notice the **vanishing point**, which can also be moved with the mouse. The two lines of perspective converge into this vanishing point.

With **Object/Clear Perspective** you can remove them at any time.

> **Hint**: to find on CorelDRAW 2020 under object, in earlier versions this effect was arranged in the Effects menu.

21.4 THE ENVELOPE EFFECT

➢ Choose the next copy of the sample text and start with **Effects/Envelope** from the tool bar left side.

➢ Now you can modify the envelope at the handles.

  ✎ NOTE: If you want a straight envelope, you can delete the turning points in the middle.

Further settings you find in the Property Bar:

Some **Presets:** rectilinear, slant, pinch…, every can then be changed as desired with the Shape Tool.

You can add or modify **turning points** as in the chapter about the form tool described.

Straight line or an **arc line** for a trumpet?

Instead Putty (elastic) you have you have these possibilities: horizontal, vertical, original:

Horizontal: the text is adapted to the envelope horizontally. Mostly illegible result.	
Original: the shape is maintained half way.	
Vertical: the text is adjusted vertically to the envelope.	

21.5 CONTOUR

Here we can create different colored steps around the object or within it. **Contour is available twice in the Effects menu**, with the upper vectorization contours, in this case the **lower** one.

➢ Select a new example text, then **Effects/Contour**:

To centre, inside or outside.

Steps = Number of contours (stripes).
Offset = Width of strips.

The normal fill and line color can be set with the mouse. The **line** and **fill color** of the object changes to this colors step by step.

Unfortunately, Corel always switches back to "in", so that an **error message** "steps too small" appears, just confirm and click again "out".

Contour outside with red text color:

With contour inside:

- **To Center**: Corel automatically creates as many contours (steps) as needed to match with the specified width (Contour offset). Therefore, the number of steps cannot be selected but only the width.
- Many steps with a small distance lead to soft color traces.
➢ Start with a contour outwards to see the effect.

The Colors:

Here you can choose the way through the color disk from object color to Contour fill color:

Straight / clockwise / counter clockwise.

The colors of the stripes change from the filling color of the object to the fill color choosed in above contour menu, same for the line color.

Possible Problems:

- Contours inwards do not seem to go if the distance is set too high! Even too think of a line makes the filling color unrecognizable.
  ↳ Possibly start with a contour outwards, in order to be able to recognize the width of the strips, then try inward.
  ↳ Increase as much as possible to see the effect, especially with a contour inward.

22. Extrusion

Finally! The classic effect. We will go through all of the settings.

> ➢ Write the sample text **EX** and set a very large font for it.
> ➢ **Copy** this text several times to have some exercise material.

> The **Edit/Aply buttons** are missing on the menu, so the **Effects/Extrude** menu on Corel 2020 will not work. Maybe this will be corrected soon in an update, we set the extrusion simply by mouse.

22.1 The Depth of the Extrusion

The setting options are divided into some menus. First the **depth**.

> ➢ Switch to extrusion on the left side of the effects, then specify the extrusion with the mouse button pressed down from the EX object:

The **vanishing point** appears as soon as we have specified the extrusion with pressed mouse button and can be moved with the mouse.

The settings in the property bar:

The perspective is very important: "Small Back" is customary, which results in a spatial effect!

Depth reduce yields beautiful shadows rather than coarse extrusions, try 1 and 5 mm.

With color the extrusion is particularly beautiful - follow immediately.

22.2 THE COLOR

Extrusions are only really beautiful with colors.

> ➢ Choose the fill color from the color palette with the left mouse click, the **line color** with the right. In addition, the color for the extruded surface can be set in the property bar on this icon:

Object fill (= same fill as object),
Solid fill (= another color as object fill),
Shade (= color gradient fill).

Sample with **Shade Fill** from red to blue by red text color.

> ➢ Try a **gradient** and set two different colors, additionally choose the appropriate object color and line color.

22.3 THE ROTATION

Objects can be rotated on the second card:

Just touch with the mouse and rotate this disc.

Rotated text with extrusion.

Enter **coordinates** for the rotation or read the coordinates out.

Resetting: Turn off the rotation.

22.4 Light and Shadow

For real objects there is always **light and shadow**. For this, we can place up to three **lamps** in Corel, which not only illuminate our object, but also create the shadow pages. Each of these lamps can be regulated by their luminosity.

In this window, you can **move** the lamps.

Too bright of lamps cause that only bright white instead of the colors is displayed; in this case, reduce the brightness!

Switch the **lamps** on or off here.

The bright area, as in a spotlight.

Dark shadow sides as in reality.

22.5 Bevels

Here sharp edges can be replaced by bevelled surfaces, which is the case with all natural objects, so that the objects become even more realistic.

For small objects, use a small bevel between 0.1 and 1 mm. Unfortunately, the extruded surface does not get a bevel.

22.6 A Title Sheet

Last exercise, a trifle: A title page for a book.

> ➢ **New drawing** with book size e.g. 23,5x17cm, set grid and **guidelines** as border lines and write **each line of text separately**, then align with the left and right guide lines.

> ➢ Then, **extrude the first line** with short depth, highlight the next line, and clone with **Object/Clone Effect/Extrude from** the extrusion of the first line (you have to click then on the extruded area). By **cloning**, changes to the original are automatically transferred to the copies.

Extrude the circle, then push the vanishing point outwards.

Put a white rectangle over the outside part to hide it.

Adapt the text with the **Envelope**-Effect to match the trumpet shape.

Set a **rectangle** behind the text with rounded corners (Property Bar) and set a thick, dashed line in the line menu.

Write this text separately so that you can set a matching shape with the **Envelope**-Effect as shown.

> ➢ At the end, draw a rectangle across the whole page to which a **color gradient fill** is assigned. Finally, place this rectangle backwards.

22.7 EXCLUSION EXERCISE: EXTRUSION

Try, at last, the following:

➢ New drawing and first set the paper format matching (how big you want to print out?), then write both text blocks separately.
➢ Turn them to the same angle and extrude 2021.
➢ If the extrusion is finished, mark the other text and **Object/Clone Effect /Extrude from**, then click on the extruded area.
  ↳ Thus, the other text has the same extrusion, possibly reducing the depth of the extrusion, since the font is smaller.
➢ Finally, draw a rectangle as large as the page, with a conical or radial color gradient filling and put it in the **background**.

Stars with the polygon drawn + Drop Shadow that was offset.

22.8 SUMMARY SHADOWS

- In the above exercise, we have created a spatial shadow through an extrusion.
- Also, remember that you can create a minimally moved copy as a shadow using **Window/Dockers/Transform** (s. p. 55).
  ↳ Assigning a different color to this copy creates a nice shadow.
  ↳ You can create a gradient shadow using the **Drop Shadow Tool**, described on page 82.
- Of course, the effect **contour** could also be used to create a soft-running shadow.

Notizen: ....

....

....

22.9 Basics

Basics:

⊃ Save cleaned up work in **Folders + Subfolders** and make **backups**!

⊃ Most important programs of CorelDraw Suite:
- **CorelDraw** (cdr): a **vector drawing program** = for presentations, covers, advertisement ..., combine photos, graphics and text here.
- **Photo-Paint** (cpt): **pixel** = dots, for photos and photo editing.
- More: **Capture** (make photos from your monitor), **Connect** choose ClipArt or Corel Web Content...

Shortcuts:

[F1]	Help
[Ctrl]-z	Undo
[Ctrl]-p	Print
[Ctrl]-x	Cut
[Ctrl]-c	Copy
[Ctrl]-v	Paste

CorelDRAW-Shortcuts:

[Alt]-y	Align on Grid on/off
[Ctrl]-a	Select all
[Ctrl]-g	Group
[Ctrl]-u	Ungroup

[Ctrl]-L	Combine	
[Ctrl]-K	Break Combination	
[Shift]-[Page up/down]	Set marked object before/behind	
[Ctrl]-t	Text Menu	
[Ctrl]-F11	Special Characters Menu	

Zoom:

[F3]	Zoom out
[F4]	Zoom marked objects
[F9]	Whole window view (back with [Esc])

23. INDEX

[

[Ctrl] 44
   -z for undo 30
[Shift] 49

A

auto replace 110

B

background 26, 81
backup 7
bars 33
baseline grid 43
bevel 129
bezier 37
bitmaps 119
business card 112

C

CAD 9
caps 109
cdr 14
change size 21
characters 60, 107
christmas card 70
circle 44
   -arc 92, 93
clipart
   -file extensions 14
   -insert 81, 83, 116
CMYK 61
color
   - scheme 61
   -color palette 28, 65
   -palettes 66
   -paper color 112
   -pick up 28
combine 94
command bars 33
compressing 10
connect 7
copy 22, 23
Corel
   -fonts 60
   -overview add-ins 8
   -photo-paint 119
   -trace 119
   -tutor 19
corner rounding 21, 130
corner sizing handles 21
cpt 14
curve editing 91–103

D

default 33
delete 21, 30
dimensions 53
display options 32
draft 32
drawing tablet 35
drawing tools 20
duplicate 23, 45

E

edit fill 65
effects
   -contour 126
   -delete 87
   -envelope 125
   -extrude 127
   -letters 124
   -perspective 124
ellipses 26
exercise
   -bars 33
   -birthday invitation 81
   -blossom 56
   -book cover 130
   -business card dog 112
   -cartonhome 72
   -characters 107
   -christmas card 70
   -color pick up 28
   -convertible 36
   -copy 23
   -drawing-basics 21
   -effects 124
   -figures 96
   -flyer 115

-grafic text 58
-guidelines 46
-house 45
-letterhead 59
-line 35
-line thickness 29
-locomotive 73
-moon 92
-paragraph text 117
-party 91
-photos inserting 116
-pick up objects 27
-pivot point 54
-pyramid squares 44
-quadrates 50
-railway wheel 54, 55
-rectangle 21
-rectangles, ellipses 26
-shadow 105
-sizing handles 21
-snake 99
-symbol font 60
-to the back 30
-truck 48
-turn text 58
-wine 83
extrude .... *see* effects

F

file
   -conversion 14
   -extension 12
   -new, open, save 19
   -save 24
filling 67–79
   -copy 78
   -fill types 76, 77
   -smart fill tool 39
fit text to path 108
flickr 80
focoltone 66
folder 7
   -new, change 24
forward/to the back 30
fotolia 79
freehand tool 35

G

grammatik checker 110
grid 43
grinding 51
group 59, 94
   -features 56
guidelines 46, 47
   -snap on 48

H

help 15
hints 15, 25

I

import/export 79
increase 31
interactive
   -filling 85
   -mesh fill 86
   -transparency 87
iStock 79

L

label print 114
letterhead 59
line 35
   -convert in curve 100
   -line thickness 29
   -polyline 37, 71
lineal 53
lines 36
lock object 81

M

mark 27
   -several objects 94
mesh fill 86
mirror 27
move 21, 22, 27
ms office 59

N

nose 95

O

Object
   -useable objects 80
overview
   -copy 23
   -corel programs 7
   -CorelDRAW 25
   -drawing tools 20
   -sizing handles 21
   -zoom 31

P

page 25, 118
   -set up 26
page size 26
page sorter view 32
painting 11
pantone 66
paper
   -color 112
   -color paper 81
   -size 26

paragraph text 111–18
parallelogram 21
pen
    -calligraphic................................ 38
    -pressure sensitive 35
pencil types 37
photo
    -brightness 119
    -cut.. 116
    -effects 119
    -import 79
    -modify..................................... 119
    -scanned..................................... 11
    -size ratio................................. 116
Photo-Paint 9, 11, 119
pick tool 20
pick up tool 27
pixel grid 43
pixel-graphics 10
planning... 8
poligon... 35
polygon... 51
polyline 71
position... 30
preconditions 7
print... 114
printable area 32
property bar 23
    -curve 95
    -interactive filling 85
    -interaktive transp. 87
    -many objects............................ 27
    -photo 119
    -text.........................57, 111, 117
    -zoom 31

Q
quadrate... 49

R
rectangles 26
redo 30
reflect 113
reshape... 71
RGB.. 61
rotate...................................... 21, 106
rounded edges 21

S
save 24

scale 53
scaling 27
shadow... 82
shape tool 70, 94
size 27
size change, skale........................... 113
smart fill tool, -drawing.................... 39
special occasions.............................. 81
spell checker 110
spiral 51
square 44
star.. 92
step width 45
stylesheet............................... *see* style
symbol font 60, 107

T
text
    -effects................................ 123–27
    -graphic................................ 105–10
    -paragraph text..................... 111–18
    -text tool 57–60
text processing................................. 12
thesaurus 110
tick snapping 108
toolbox...................................... 20, 33
transparency 87
Transparency 80, 88
turn 27
typographic quotes......................... 110

U
undo.. 30
unit.. 53
units 26

V
vanishing point............................... 127
vector graphics.................................. 9
vektor-pixel comparison 11

W
welcome screen 19
wingdings 107
wmf... 59
workspace... 8

Z
zero point.. 53
zoom 31, 32

Made in the USA
Monee, IL
07 September 2021